From Anger to Intimacy

DR. GARY SMALLEY
TED CUNNINGHAM

From ANGER to INTIMACY

How Forgiveness Can Transform Your Marriage

Regal

From Gospel Light
Ventura, California, U.S.A.

Published by Regal
From Gospel Light
Ventura, California, U.S.A.
www.regalbooks.com
Printed in the U.S.A.

Library of Congress Cataloging-in-Publication Data
Smalley, Gary.
From anger to intimacy : understanding anger and the freedom of forgiveness /
Gary Smalley and Ted Cunningham.
p. cm.
ISBN 978-0-8307-4676-7 (hard cover)
1. Marriage—Religious aspects—Christianity. 2. Anger—Religious aspects—Christianity.
3. Forgiveness—Religious aspects—Christianity. I. Cunningham, Ted. II. Title.
BV835.S5525 2009
248.4—dc22
2008017147

1 2 3 4 5 6 7 8 9 10 / 15 14 13 12 11 10 09

Rights for publishing this book outside the U.S.A. or in non-English languages are administered by Gospel Light Worldwide, an international not-for-profit ministry. For additional information, please visit www.glww.org, e-mail info@glww.org, or write to Gospel Light Worldwide, 1957 Eastman Avenue, Ventura, CA 93003, U.S.A.

I (Gary) want to dedicate this book to my daughter,
Kari, and my daughters-in-law, Amy Smalley and Erin Smalley,
who continually provide a wonderful example of how an
extended family lives, plays and worships together in complete
forgiveness and love toward each other.

I (Ted) want to dedicate this book to two great churches:
Woodland Hills Community Church and The River.
Both have contributed to my life in big ways.
I will forever be indebted to them.

Contents

Acknowledgments

We would like to thank Roger Gibson for dreaming with us and making *From Anger to Intimacy* a reality. He serves as more than our literary agent; he is also a great friend.

Margaret Feinberg is much more than just a writer. She is a great collaborator with a journalistic style that draws the best out of us. Margaret is a servant and an incredible wordsmith.

A big thank you to Alex Field and Kim Bangs for leading this book from start to finish at Regal. They have been so encouraging and are a pure delight to work with.

Thank you, Regal and Gospel Light! Bill Greig III, you lead your team with excellence. Also, a big thanks goes to the team, including Deena Davis, Bill Denzel, Bruce Barbour, Mark Weising, Aly Hawkins and the marketing and sales teams at Regal Books!

We also want to say thank you to all of the staff at the Smalley Relationship Center. Day in and day out, you serve marriages around the world. Your hard work does not go unnoticed. Thank you.

Thank you, Norma Smalley, Terry Brown, Ron Cunningham, Bonnie Cunningham, Sue Parks and Roger Gibson for reading the manuscript and offering great insight.

The staff at Woodland Hills Community Church played a big part in this book. Ted Burden is my colleague and trusted friend. Bernard Bourque offered many valuable teaching insights. Pam Strayer transcribed, and Denise Bevins handled so many details of my life during the process. Richard Williams and Jim Brawner helped with the creative process. Thank you! Thank you! Thank you!

To all of our family and friends, many of whom have stories that fill these pages, we love you and owe you a debt of gratitude for the patience in this process.

1

You Don't Have to Live that Way Anymore

It was a storybook wedding. The bride wore an elegant white dress. The groom donned a traditional black tuxedo. The bridesmaids strolled gracefully down the aisle. The flower girl and ring bearer were wide-eyed and earned coos and giggles from the crowd. The flowers were beautiful. The music played harmoniously. The candles added just the right hues to the backdrop of the ceremony.

The joy, elation and excitement of the day left Sabrina with an unmistakable glow. Within a few moments, she and Johnny had made the commitment to love, honor, cherish and respect each other in sickness and in health, for richer or for poorer, until death did them part.

But less than 36 months later, both Johnny and Sabrina were ready to break their covenant of marriage and file for divorce. How did something that began so perfectly grow into an unhealthy, hurtful relationship?

The transformation began shortly after the honeymoon. When the young couple walked into my office for counseling, I (Ted) remember sensing the pain, hurt and disappointment in their eyes as they began recounting their stories and interactions. Sabrina remembered one evening shortly after they were married:

"I'm going out tonight, honey," Johnny announced on his way out the door. "I'm hanging with the boys. I'll be home around midnight."

"What do you mean you are going out tonight?" Sabrina protested. "I had a special meal planned."

"Don't you remember last week, when I told you that Craig is hosting a Texas hold 'em tournament tonight?" Johnny answered.

"Yes, I remember you mentioning it, but I don't remember us making any decisions about it."

"What . . . are you my mother?" Johnny snapped.

"No, but I thought it would be cool if we hung out tonight, because we're out every other night this week with work, church and my parents' get-together."

"Baby, I can't let the guys down. They're expecting me. I'll try to get home a little earlier, if that will make you happy."

"Fine, I'll see you in the morning."

"Now you're mad?" Johnny asked.

"Go!"

With that, Johnny left the house. Six months later, the marriage was deteriorating on multiple levels. Sabrina's small annoying habits were growing too big for Johnny to overlook. Meanwhile, Johnny's lack of attention to detail or care for hygiene were becoming more than Sabrina could handle. Instead of talking to her husband, Sabrina spent long hours on the phone each night criticizing him. She picked on the way Johnny ate and belittled him for not doing more around the house.

One night, Sabrina was so fed up with Johnny that she went upstairs with a basket of freshly dried clothes that needed to be folded. She sat on the couch next to Johnny and picked up one article of clothing at a time. If it was her garment, she neatly folded and placed it on the floor next to the basket. If it was his, she threw it at him and said, "Fold it your @#%& self!"

The couples' communication was nearly nonexistent, and both spouses were suffering. What began as irritation quickly ballooned into annoyance, which resulted in feelings of being disrespected, devalued and controlled. Anger filled their home.

Whenever anger takes up residence in a marriage, sexual intimacy moves out. Anger is like a vacuum; it sucks the tenderness, gentleness and honor out of the relationship. As a result, Johnny and Sabrina quickly lost interest in each other sexually. Though they continued to sleep in the same bed, they never went to bed at the same time. This became the new norm for their relationship.

Nearly two years passed before Johnny came home with bad news: He had been fired from his job as a teacher in the local school district.

"They caught me looking at porn on the computer at school," Johnny confessed.

Sabrina was shocked. *What are we going to do for money?* she wondered. *What are people going to say?*

Then an even more devastating thought struck her: *How long has this been going on?*

Johnny's addiction to pornography had started in high school and progressed through college. Though he struggled with it while dating Sabrina and then during their engagement, he kept telling himself, *Once we get married, everything will be all right.*

Everything was all right for the first few weeks. But then the relationship soured, and Johnny returned to his old addiction.

He sat across the dining room table from Sabrina, waiting for his wife to unleash her fury. But instead, tears began welling up in her eyes.

"I have something I need to tell you," Sabrina stammered. "Remember Jack from high school?"

"Yeah," Johnny said, feeling a nervous tightness in his chest.

"Well, when I opened up my Facebook account online about a year ago, we reconnected. At first it was just a few emails back and forth, but then we met for coffee."

Johnny's mind raced with questions: *Did that meeting happen on one of my poker nights? Did I drive her to this guy?* But he managed to hold them inside.

Johnny asked the question he feared most: "Did you sleep with him?"

"No, but we kissed," Sabrina answered.

Then there was silence.

How could Sabrina and Johnny possibly hold their marriage together with such distrust? How could they move beyond the anger and disappointment they felt? How could they build a new foundation for their marriage?

Sabrina's anger toward Johnny's addiction and Johnny's anger toward Sabrina's kissing an old friend are healthy responses. Any normal person would react with shock and anger. At the same time, now they both needed to make choices to resolve their anger in a healthy way. (I'm happy to tell you that they did work hard to rebuild their marriage relationship, and they did learn the life-giving principles of dealing with their destructive anger issues—the same principles that we will present in the rest of this book.)

Admittedly, Sabrina and Johnny's life had enough twists and turns to be an Everyman story. Their marriage relationship took more hits in a few short years than most marriages will experience in a lifetime. But even if your marriage is visited only with simple problems such as differences in views about housecleaning, the chances are that you will deal with enough irritations and occasional anger flare-ups with your spouse that you can benefit from the proven tactics we will share.

In fact, it's often the small, daily irritations experienced over a long period of time, and not dealt with in a healthy way, that have the power to strain a marriage and lead to estrangement. That is true probably because feelings of irritation can lead to resentment and anger in marriage that continue to build below the surface, regardless of the face you or your spouse present to each other every day. And that's a danger zone.

So, even if you would say that your marriage is good, is more than good, or it couldn't be better, you can benefit by learning the secrets to anger control and how you can create closeness in your communication with your mate. Even if there is no problem looming in your marriage right now, you need this information, because you live in a fallen world with other fallen human beings who will rub you the wrong way, and vice versa.

We have stories to tell you from our own lives of how we learned to respond to some big trials and some smaller irritations, and we have proven strategies to give you that will greatly benefit your interactions with those you come in contact with, beginning with the person closest to you.

Anger: A God-given Emotion

If there's only one thing you take away from this book, we want you to understand that anger in and of itself is not a bad thing; anger is an emotion designed by and given to you by God; *but it's what you do with that anger that can negatively affect your spiritual, mental and emotional health.*

Anger is not a bad emotion. Think about it: If you cannot feel anger toward evil, then it stands to reason that you cannot love what is good. In other words, there are some things that it's okay to get angry about. God wants you to be angry about some things, such as social injustice. He feels the anger, too. But even when we get upset about the right, constructive, purposeful things, we still must make sure we handle anger in the appropriate way.

Unfortunately, anger is not just sparked by good, right and constructive things. Anger can be triggered by rejection, judgment, failure, control or lack of control, neglect, loneliness or inferiority. If someone is abandoned or left out, cheated or mistreated, overlooked or misunderstood, the result is often anger. No matter what the cause, when left unresolved, anger will lead to sin. Anger will sprout jealousy, envy, strife and contention.

Scientists have even discovered that stress, which is often caused by unresolved anger, releases a chemical in your brain called *cortisol*, which can damage your brain and cause your nervous system to shut down. If left unchecked, anger can result not only in physical disease but also in emotional and spiritual disease. Anger may be taking a bigger toll on your relationships and life than you realize.

The path of anger looks something like this:

Event→Emotion→Anger→Sin

Anger is not a primary emotion; it is a secondary one. You feel a host of other emotions before anger, such as the feeling of being devalued, cheated, invalidated, unloved, neglected, controlled, disrespected, disconnected, belittled, judged, abandoned or a like a failure. Planted and watered over time, those emotions are like seeds that take root in your heart and grow into anger. Anger left unresolved produces poison that ultimately kills and destroys everything in its path.

Every day, you experience a host of encounters or events that produce an emotion in you. If you feel wronged or overlooked or unfairly treated, anger will often surface. When the anger is left unresolved, it festers inside of you like an infection, until it eventually leads to sin. That's why it's so important to deal with the resulting emotion and anger quickly, before it results in sin or further self-destructive behavior.

In chapter 2, we will begin to explore how you can bring anger to a healthy end. We believe there are three main outlets for anger: You can (1) *stuff it*, (2) *spew it* or (3) *study it*. The good news is that if you *study* anger, you can learn to resolve conflict, hurt and pain in a healthy way, no matter what event or action has seemingly come against you. This second chapter will provide some of the foundational tools you will need in order to experience peace and satisfaction in the midst of life's unexpected and unsettling fluctuations.

In chapter 3, we go inside the cycle of anger to examine not only what anger looks like but also how you can break out of it. Whether you realize it or not, you have internal buttons that, when pushed, release anger, frustration and even rage. You can learn to recognize and master these buttons. They do not have to get the best of you or your relationships. How do Gary and I know? Because we've personally wrestled with our buttons, and we're finding more freedom and grace in this area than we ever thought possible—and so can you!

More than anything, we believe that it's essential for you to take responsibility and ownership of the anger in your life—no matter how small or big the outbursts. That's why in chapter 4 we give you specific tactics to deal with anger and rage when these emotions rear their ugly heads. You can get a grip on your responses and make sure that anger doesn't get a grip on you. Even if you don't think of yourself as a person with "anger issues," you might be surprised to discover what's lurking in your heart.

In chapter 5, we will examine some principles that may go against what you were taught in the church. The messages of "don't let your heart be your guide" and "you can't trust your emotions" have been interpreted as "don't take care of your heart." We want to teach you how to nurture your emotions and guard your heart, because it is your guide. Proverbs 4:23 calls it "the wellspring of life." All of life flows from your heart.

In chapter 6, we look at what it means not just to forgive but also to embrace a spirit of forgiveness. Did you know that forgiveness can become a lifestyle? When you forgive, you not only set the other person free but you also become a little bit freer yourself. In order to walk in the freedom God intends for you, it's important to recognize the three essentials of forgiveness as well as five keys to nurturing a forgiving spirit.

Then, in chapter 7, we will challenge you to put the act of forgiving and being forgiven into practice in "Restoration: Crafting the Perfect Apology." Do you ever struggle with what to say when you offer an apology to someone? If so, you're not alone. While almost everyone knows how to say, "I'm sorry," very few people know how to deliver a sincere, heartfelt apology that works as a balm to the oldest and deepest of wounds. In this chapter, we give you five tools for crafting the best apologies—the kind that will revolutionize your relationships.

Once you know how to craft the perfect apology, we give you a chance to put that apology into practice in chapter 8. In "Unrelenting: Roadblocks to Forgiveness," we look at the nine roadblocks to forgiveness and give you tactics to remove them once and for all from your life. You'll also be asked to look at the final 15 minutes of your life and develop a forgiveness list that will change your life and your relationships forever.

You may be reading along and thinking that all of this is good advice for someone else, but your situation is too difficult. Maybe you're thinking that your marriage is beyond repair. If so, you won't want to miss chapter 9! We tackle dealing with a difficult spouse and look at four life-changing keys to forgiving him or her to make your marriage work no matter where your spouse is spiritually.

In chapter 10, we look at the six requirements for breaking sexual addiction and how you and your spouse can heal after an affair. Then in chapter 11, we explore the dangers of unresolved anger in your marriage. You will learn three valuable ways to foster forgiveness, as well as six ways you can maintain forgiveness in your marriage.

Finally, in chapter 12, we'll answer some of the "biggie" questions you have about anger and forgiveness in your marriage and relationships.

The good news is that you don't have to let anger or unforgiveness rob you of the life you are meant to live. By learning how to nurture a spirit of forgiveness, you can become all God means for you to be in your marriage, with your family and other relationships, and in your reactions to life.

In the upcoming pages, we will show you the kind of transformation that anyone can experience when he or she truly understands the power of forgiveness.

So get ready to dive in. First, we will examine and expose the roots of anger and identify healthy responses to what we feel. This is a foundational chapter you won't want to miss.

From GarySmalley.com

Each week we receive emails to our website, GarySmalley.com, from people with questions about their struggling marriages. We do our best to answer these questions with biblical truth and practical insight. Be sure to read through the various scenarios at the end of each chapter and our suggested guidelines for resolution.

Q: *I live in constant anger toward my wife. I need help with understanding and channeling my anger well. Where do I start?*

A: Begin by recognizing that anger is an indicator of something else at work. Anger is an emotion. Like all of our emotions, there's nothing wrong with it in and of itself. Anger is our human response to something that occurs or, at least, to our perception of that occurrence. In fact, some anger is good; we get angry when we see an injustice or when someone is trying to violate our personal boundary lines. In such cases, our anger is what motivates us to take appropriate action. But after anger motivates us to do something good, we can't afford to let it linger inside us. We have to get it out. Anger is a good emotion when it gets us moving; but if we let anger take root, we set ourselves up for a great deal of potential harm.

No matter how many times you try to resolve those issues or enter into deeper intimacy, the anger below the surface can keep you in turmoil. Living with angry people is like living in a minefield. If you say or do the wrong thing, *kaboom!* They explode all over everyone. And you're left thinking, *I had no idea that one thing I did would cause such a reaction.*

Actually, anger is a secondary emotion, not a primary feeling. It arises out of *fear, frustration, hurt* or some combination of these. For example, if someone says something harsh to us, we first feel hurt and then anger.

When we strip the word "anger" down to its deepest level, we see the thread of unfulfilled expectations. Frustration comes when we don't receive what we had expected from other people or from circumstances. When you get frustrated or feel hurt, immediately go to God and tell Him about it. Replace your feelings of anger with more of Him.

2

Recognize

Identifying Where Anger Appears

Anger can appear in us unexpectedly, at any time, in any place. In this chapter, we will take a candid look at anger as it lingers hidden below the surface, in our hearts, our lives and our relationships. We will explore the three outlets of anger—stuffing it, spewing it and studying it—and teach you two questions to ask yourself that have the power to change your life and relationships for the good. This chapter also includes a practical quiz to help you recognize your anger issues and responses and identify whether they are healthy or unhealthy. All of us must learn how to resolve anger and refuse to allow it to take root beneath the surface of our life.

The Anger Buoy

Unresolved anger is like a buoy held underwater. It may hide below the surface for days, weeks, months or even years, but sooner or later it will pop up to the surface. Unresolved anger may not surface in the same way or at the same place as it has in the past, but it *will* eventually reappear.

I (Ted) have experienced this surfacing of anger in my own life. The story I'm about to tell you is not primarily an example about my marriage; but my wife, Amy, went through these events with me, and she was affected by my anger responses and what I learned as a result of the pain we experienced together. As I learned how to deal with my below-the-surface anger, long practiced as a first response whenever I feel hurt or threatened, I also learned how to restructure those responses in healthy ways. The patterns I learned with the help of Gary's mentoring have completely changed my life and my relationships, and have provided me with a flourishing marriage and a healthy way to respond to my children.

You could say that Gary and I have an almost "evangelistic fervor" about the message of how to turn anger to intimacy, and we are eager to share it with you because we now live the truth of this message in our own marriages. We're not perfect, but we've learned how to keep short accounts and maintain a spirit of forgiveness with our mates, no matter what life throws at us. Compared to the way I used to think and react, what God has worked in me has brought unbelievable freedom! Gary would say the same, for he learned these truths before I did. Through examples from our lives and the lives of others, we will show you how to get to that place so that you, too, can experience increased joy and intimacy in your marriage.

What once had the power to create in me debilitating anger now rebounds against a heart of gratefulness that I would never have believed possible. The details of my story are specific to my life, but they contain principles that are directly applicable to your life. Because, chances are, you will also sustain a devastating event or series of events that will require some serious study of your anger responses in order to overcome them. You, too, will be given an opportunity, at some point, to learn from a painful relational experience.

So let what happened to me carry you a bit further along in your understanding of how to find your path from anger to intimacy.

The event that changed how I process what happens to me, and how I respond to what is said to me, was the most painful experience of my life so far; but I can now say that it was the best thing that ever happened to me.

Life Is "Good"

At the age of 26, I became the senior pastor of a 400-member church in southwest Missouri. As a recent graduate of seminary, I had no idea that I was headed for the single most painful year of my life. I was fresh out of school, married to Amy and ready to change the world. My passion was the Church and helping people who had given up on the Church find their way back. I had the book smarts, a few years of experience as an associate pastor and a heart full of dreams and goals. But there was one thing missing in my education and experience: pain.

In short, I was formally trained but not molded; knowledgeable but not fully equipped; puffed up but lacking in love. The first year as a senior pastor taught me the following:

- I was authoritarian in my leadership style rather than authoritative.
- I led from a *closed* posture rather than an *open* posture.
- I was highly defensive.
- I did not accept the opinions of others.
- It was my way or the highway.

(Worst of all, I had learned some of these practices while in seminary.)

This church was an exceptional church in many ways. Hundreds of people with no church background walked through the doors for the first time each year. The staff was real and open to my dreams and leadership. The founding pastor was dearly loved and his passion for Jesus was reflected in the church. I was to become the church's second pastor in its short six-year history.

Life Is "Bad"

About five months after I accepted the position as senior pastor, one of the other pastors asked me to lunch. I didn't notice anything unusual about the request or his tone.

"Yeah, man, where do you want to go?" I responded.

The pastor suggested a fast-food sandwich shop nearby. Like an ostrich with his head in the sand, I didn't think twice when he invited another key leader from our staff to join us. I had no idea that I was walking into one of the worst lunches of my life.

Munching on a toasted chicken sandwich and chips, I took a gulp of my soda when one of the pastors dropped a bombshell I'll never forget: "Ted, we think you would make a great small-groups pastor."

I looked up from my drink and thought, *Did you—my friend and colleague—just say what I think you just said?* I looked at him, puzzled.

"We just think the senior pastor is not the best job position for you," he continued.

I could feel my body tensing. My eyes widened. My jaw dropped slightly. I could feel the adrenaline flowing through my veins. I took a quiet, tense breath and listened as these two pastors—men I had encouraged, challenged, loved and served—offered a laundry list of reasons why I should not be the leader of the church:

- *You have the book knowledge of leadership, but not the experience.*
- *Your teaching is geared toward believers, and we need a more seeker-oriented speaker.*
- *You don't seem to be open to feedback. You are authoritarian in your leadership approach.*

The only thing worse than hearing the raw list of faults was proving them right in my response. Whenever my buttons are pushed, my reactions include *withdrawal*, a *defensive posture* and *sarcasm*. In other words, when my lower lip starts quivering and my statements are short, jabbing and defensive, you know my buttons have been pushed. What are my buttons? Glad you asked.

- I do not like to be controlled.
- I do not want to be judged.
- I do not want to feel like a failure.

That five-minute conversation pushed all three buttons at once. I was stewing inside. I was mad. No, "mad" is not a strong enough word—I was *irate*. But I kept quiet and let them share their hearts. (After all, my first reaction is always withdrawal.)

When it was my turn to respond, I looked at the men across the table and, trying desperately to keep the tone of my voice calm, said, "I would like both of you to resign."

They were making ridiculous, preposterous and outlandish statements, and getting rid of my coworkers would make this all go away. Or so I thought. At the time, I couldn't hear their words. Worse, I couldn't bear the truth that they were right on every account. By the end of our time together, my stomach was in a knot, my jaw was clenched and I was doing everything I knew to keep from losing my cool.

In God's providence and wisdom, there were three major flaws in my request for their resignation. First, the by-laws of the church did not give me the right to fire these leaders or ask them to resign. Second, I underestimated how much these two staff members—who had faithfully served at the church for years—were dearly loved and supported by the leadership and congregation. Finally, I overestimated my own talent and skills.

That lunch was a turning point in my life, my ministry and my marriage. The aftermath of that meeting was felt for months both in our church and in our home, because as I worked through the anger in my heart, I began to see my marriage transform. I improved my ability to communicate with Amy, to love her and to serve her like I never had before.

This church conflict brought Amy and me together as a team. As a pastor, it is easy for the church to become a "mistress." After all, you spend all of your time consumed with thoughts about her, and your marriage and family get the leftovers. During this time, our communication went to new levels because I felt that she was the only one I had left. I discovered firsthand that when we learn to deal with anger issues wherever they surface, we practice skills that help us handle our anger wherever we go.

Through this difficult experience, I met Gary Smalley. He became my mentor. In the end, he saved both my ministry and my marriage. Gary shared so many deep truths about anger and forgiveness that my life and relationships were transformed. Today I thank God for the most painful experience of my life that was brought to me by this church. It truly was the best thing that ever happened to me, and Gary and I will share with you the lessons I learned from that experience.

I (Gary) remember when I first met Ted and his wife, Amy. He was a young man full of energy and life, and I could tell that he truly loved the Lord. However, his rudder was useless because the wind was out of his sail. The first time he shared about his experiences at his church, he carefully chose every word, trying to avoid saying the wrong thing. From the tone of his voice and the strain with which he spoke, I knew he was angry. His joy for ministry was gone.

I could tell that Amy was also wounded. This didn't surprise me: Pastors' wives often take the hit even harder than their husbands. Through tear-filled eyes, she explained the hurt and confusion about how a church could love them one month and want them to leave the next.

As Ted and Amy shared their heartache with me, I sensed that deep down, Ted believed that he had been wronged. We could have focused on discussing the hierarchy of church leadership and theology, but it was not the time or place. The focus of our initial lunch needed to be on helping Ted and Amy find forgiveness. Ted, in particular, had unresolved anger. It was as if he was drinking the poison of unforgiveness and hoping that his staff would get sick. That morning, I started on a journey with Ted that continues to this day.

What I saw in his life as he began to let go of his anger and to nurture forgiveness in his life was true transformation. It's the kind of transformation I've seen in thousands of lives through my seminars and books on this topic. You would be amazed at just how prevalent the issue of anger is for both men and women.

So often when we think of anger in a relationship, it's linked to physical abuse, which is destructive, harmful and, at times, even life-threatening. But anger does not have to manifest itself as physical to be dangerous. That's why discovering how to deal with anger and unforgiveness is so crucial. Without the skills and lessons explored in this book, anger can strip you of everything you love, everything that's most important to you.

When I heard that Gary wanted to help, I thought, *Great! Gary Smalley, the world's relationship expert, is going to give me proven strategies to fix the problems at this church. He is going to*

help straighten out the staff, adjust the structure of the church and chase off the leadership.

I was wrong. Gary did no such thing.

During our first breakfast meeting, he helped me examine my heart. "Start from the beginning, Ted," he said. "I want to hear everything that happened."

About halfway through my story about the struggles and difficulties I was facing, Gary started to smile and to praise God—out loud. I remember looking at Amy and thinking, *Gary Smalley is not the guy I thought he was. Why is he enjoying my pain so much?*

"Continue," Gary finally said, after enjoying a hearty chuckle.

After I had poured out my heart, sharing the naked truth that I had never felt more like a failure in my entire life and that I was wrestling with evil thoughts toward my co-workers, Gary said something that changed my life and ministry outlook forever: "Ted, do you have any idea how blessed you are? Most guys wait 5 to 10 years after seminary to get this beating, and you have been blessed to get it in the first 5 months. If I put $100,000 on this table, it couldn't pay for the education you are getting. All I can think of is that God has very big plans for you, and He is letting you go through this advanced graduate class to get there. He is raising your threshold of pain."

I have never forgotten those words, because they forever changed how I view adversity. Through that conversation, I realized that the situation was not only a *defining* moment but also that God intended it to be a *refining* moment in my life that would forever change me to look more like Him.

After that conversation, I made a conscious decision that no matter what happened, I didn't want anger to become a part of my DNA. I didn't want anger to be my new pet. By studying my anger, I discovered the keys to overcoming anger rather than being overcome by it.

I will touch on what happened to me and to my wife and what I learned in the ensuing months and years throughout the rest of this book. There are times when I have to remind myself of what I have already learned about the way to deal with anger responses; and I'll let you in on some of those times. You will also appreciate the transparency that Gary demonstrates in the stories he shares from his own 40-plus years of marriage.

Your Life

I don't know what life experiences or tragedies have planted seeds of anger in you. I don't know the source of your betrayal, hurt or disappointment. But I do know that there is a way to get rid of those seeds of anger, and that it all relates to forgiveness. No matter what has happened to you or been done to you, you need to forgive—not for other peoples' sake, but for your own. And you need to forgive for the sake of those closest to you—especially for the sake of your spouse. We will put rubber to the road in the second half of this book to show you more about understanding and practicing biblical forgiveness. So hold on to that thought!

Unharnessed anger can destroy. It can destroy a couple's trust in each other, and it can destroy a home, a church or a community. Unresolved anger affects everyone we love, including our children and our relationship with God. There is such a thing as holy anger—being angry at the right things. But we are going to discuss unholy anger, which keeps us from becoming conformed to the image of Christ—the true path to intimacy with our spouse. We are going to discover how to put an end to anger and learn to resolve our conflict, hurt and pain in a healthy way. First, let's consider the three main ways that people deal with anger.

The Three Outlets of Anger

As we mentioned in chapter 1, anger has only three outlets. You can: (1) stuff it, (2) spew it, or (3) study it. Only the third option is healthy, but let's look at each option in turn with some examples.

Stuffing Anger

I (Ted) am a stuffer. When Amy and I enter into disagreement, it usually goes something like this:

"Don't shake your keys at me," says my wife as I stand at the end of the hall, hastening her to the car by rattling the keys ever so slightly.

"We're going to be late," I reply.

"There's a lot to do before we can get out of the house," she reminds me as she heads for the car.

That interchange is usually followed by driving a mile or two in silence. Then it doesn't matter what Amy says next, because my response is always the same: "I don't want to talk about this right now." These words are the battle cry of the stuffer. We never want to talk about it. We hope that by ignoring the situation, it may go away.

But stuffers tend to keep unresolved issues and anger like small pets.

A couple of months ago, Amy and I went out to buy a pet for our five-year-old daughter, Corynn. We had progressed beyond the $.28 Wal-Mart goldfish and knew it was time to take it to the next level.

We drove more than an hour away to visit a large pet store and were greeted by a nice lady with a huge smile who obviously loved animals. I explained that we wanted to buy a hamster for our daughter, Corynn, who was standing there smiling from ear to ear.

The lady recommended that we consider buying a guinea pig.

I was intrigued. We had never thought about a guinea pig. "What are the advantages?" I asked.

She went into all kinds of details, but the highlight was that guinea pigs don't bite. That sounded pretty good, but I knew I needed to ask the single most important question when buying a small rodent: "How long will it live?"

"Usually four or five years, but sometimes they can live up to eight years," she said with a perky smile.

"Um, that's not really what I'm looking for," I replied. "Do you have anything with a 6- to 12-month life span?"

"Maybe you're not ready for a pet," she answered firmly.

"I know *I'm* not ready for a pet," I responded. "But my daughter is!"

We walked out of the pet store with a guinea pig (Mr. Snuggle Buggles), a spinning wheel, wood chips, food and a very happy daughter.

Fast-forward one month. Corynn was no longer playing with Mr. Snuggle Buggles, and when you don't socialize a guinea pig, they get aggressive. When Corynn finally reached in the cage to pull Mr. Snuggle Buggles out, he bit her and drew blood.

When I saw the blood, Mr. Snuggle Buggles went from adorable pet to annoying rodent. I was angry, and in my anger, I told my daughter, "We are not going to keep him any longer." I called the local vet and told him the story. There was no way I was going to care for this little furry creature for the next 7 years and 11 months. I drove to the vet's office and handed Mr. Snuggle Buggles over to the attendant, trusting that the furry creature would find a good home.

On the drive back to our house, I began to see a parallel between the guinea pig and unresolved anger. Many people harbor anger like a pet. It quietly lives with them and becomes part of their lifestyle.

You can still function with unresolved anger in your heart. You can go to work, get a paycheck, raise kids, work around the house and even maintain a marriage, but like our neglected guinea pig, it will only be a matter of time before unresolved anger bites you. How is it possible to keep anger alive when you're not even aware of its presence? How do you unknowingly feed and grow anger? By rehearsing the same incident or encounter again and again in your mind. Years after the original offense, you still feel the same emotions when you think about it. You nurture and grow anger with thoughts and responses you should have given up long ago.

How do you unknowingly feed and grow anger? By rehearsing the same incident or encounter again and again in your mind. Years after the original offense, you still feel the same emotions when you think about it.

A guinea pig usually lives less than five years, but anger can live a lot longer. In fact, unresolved anger can live as long as a dog, cat or even an elephant. (I had a friend in Atlanta who had a cat that lived to be 27 years old. I am not kidding! Toward the end, the little furry friend was on chemotherapy, fighting cancer for what must have been its ninth life.) Whether you realize it or not, anger can live for decades. Like a parrot that lives more than 75 years, anger can be harbored and nurtured for a lifetime.

For those who are tempted to harbor anger, the Bible offers a valuable piece of wisdom when it instructs, "Do not be quickly provoked in your spirit, for anger resides [rests, sits, hangs out] in the lap of fools" (Eccles. 7:9). I (Ted) have committed this verse to memory because I am a stuffer. I hope that if I don't deal with something, it will magically go away. Though I know consciously that unresolved issues never just disappear, I still find myself tempted to stuff them.

If you are a stuffer like me, take the words of the apostle Paul to heart and "get rid of" anger, rage, malice and strife of all kinds (see Eph. 4:31). Unresolved anger keeps you from growing in your relationship with God. It prevents you from being the best husband or wife you can be, from being the best dad or mom you can be, and from being the person God created you to be. Worst of all, it does not allow you to reflect the righteousness of God (see Jas. 1:19-20).

Spewing Anger

A few years ago, I called two close friends to go to a late-night IMAX show after my kids went to bed. The theater was almost full, and we found seats together toward the front. There were about 400 people, including at least a hundred kids, stuffed into this IMAX theater, ready to watch *Fantastic Four: Rise of the Silver Surfer*. There was not enough room to have "the guy seat" between my friends and me, so we had to sit right next to each other, which always makes men uncomfortable.

A man toward the front had begun to explain the size of the IMAX screen to the audience when a man walked in with a two-year-old and a four-year-old. They took their seats directly in front of us and began to snack on some popcorn, a drink and a box of candy. Once the kids were situated, the man walked back to the end of the aisle, where a 280-pound man wearing a sleeveless jersey was sitting. The father of the two little boys clocked the big guy right in the jaw.

I couldn't believe my eyes. The guy who threw the punch was no more than 160 pounds, and I thought, *Why would such a scrawny guy pick a fight with someone so much bigger and not have backup?* The two men exchanged blows directly in front of us while both the guys' kids screamed their heads off. Onlookers grabbed the children to get them out of the way. I had never seen anything like it in our family town of Branson, Missouri.

The scene erupted into mayhem when a klutzy guy sitting a few rows back decided to dive into the fight and landed on the floor between the two men. A dad with three kids nearby yelled, "Bleepedy, bleepedy, bleepedy! Knock it off guys, we got kids here!" I remember thinking about that guy, *This fight makes about as much sense as you using that kind of language in front of the kids.*

Just as a manager finally started down the aisle, the woman with the bigger guy yelled, "Everyone in this theater who is using their cell phone to call the police needs to stop! Don't call the police. We will sit somewhere else!"

I have no idea what started that fight. As I went to bed that night, I thought, *I wonder what that guy at the end of the aisle could have said to cause the scrawny guy to clock him in the jaw. Did he say something inappropriate? Did he spill the guy's popcorn or drink? What could have happened that was worth starting a fistfight?*

Whenever I meet an angry man in public, my mind goes immediately to his wife. Is he loving her? Does she feel safe and protected in his home? Does he offer her words of affirmation each day? Have his fists ever found their way onto her face or body?

Whether anger manifests itself in
sharp words or punching fists, spewing anger
will poison your relationships.

I recently reenacted this fight in the theater for some of the youth in our church. I asked them, "Why do you think these two grown men fought?" The kids didn't have an answer. While no one will know the tipping point of the conflict, I do know one thing: Those fists found all their energy from unresolved anger.

Some people are tempted to stuff their anger, but others are tempted to spew it. The spewing may come in the form of verbal or physical aggression, but whether anger manifests itself in sharp words or punching fists, spewing anger will poison a relationship.

Are you struggling with your spouse because he or she is constantly angry? Do you go out of your way to avoid contact? Do you feel like you have to walk on eggshells when you're with him or her? Do you fear for your own safety or the safety of your family when you're with him or her? If so, your spouse probably spews anger, and his or her anger bucket is almost full.

"You can tell how full someone's bucket is by how often they explode and how intense the explosions are."

The Bible says that "an angry man stirs up dissention, and a hot tempered one commits many sins" (Prov. 29:22).

In other words, spewing anger undermines the marriage relationship. A spouse who spews anger can destroy his or her marriage. A family member who spews anger can ruin a holiday gathering. A coworker who spews anger can subvert the success of a business.

Scripture goes as far as to instruct, "Do not make friends with a hot tempered man, do not associate with one easily angered, or you may learn his ways and get yourself ensnared" (Prov. 22:24-25). In other words, spewing anger is contagious. If you spend too much time with someone who spews anger, it won't be too long until you begin spewing yourself. And eventually, you will spew on your spouse!

Studying Anger

In the summer of 2003, Amy and I started studying the source of our fights. We had been married at that point for seven years and had not found resolution in many areas. So we got in the habit of getting out a piece of paper (usually a placemat at restaurants) to map out the how and the why of the conflict in our marriage.

It was awkward at first, but we learned so much about each other, including how to better care for each other and our hearts. We will show you the map of our fights in the next chapter, but here is how our habit of studying anger got started.

Amy and I grew up in very different families with very different ideas about spending and saving money. Finding a mutually satisfying approach to finances had been a struggle from the beginning of our marriage. The two of us were having dinner one night when I started to share with Amy my frustrations about our money issues. That dinner conversation was rough, but it started us on the best journey of our life—a journey that has ended almost all escalated arguments in our marriage. (Notice I said "almost." As students, we should never stop learning.)

Now, before we get to the actual process of studying your anger and conflicts, I need to give you some encouragement and a warning.

First, the warning: *Understand that the process will at times be awkward.* That awkwardness comes from changing old habits of communication. You have adapted to a communication style over your lifetime, and trying a new communication style won't be fun. But the payoff is huge.

Second, *keep trying.* Practice makes perfect. You and your spouse need to give each other credit for effort.

Third, *revise as you go.* Stick it out for the long haul. Six years later, Amy and I are still tweaking our map because we learn new things about each other all the time. Use a pencil, not a pen; you will need to make changes. For example, Amy and I had once listed my primary buttons as *being controlled, being judged* and *feeling like a failure,* as I stated earlier in this chapter. It wasn't until we built a house in 2007 that I realized I had a major "being cheated" button. I was cool when the subcontractor showed up late or did not finish the job on time; but when he handed me a bill charging me for time he was not on the job, I freaked. I had not discovered the *being cheated* button, because Amy had never given me cause in our marriage.

I am convinced that studying anger, starting with the exercise of identifying and openly admitting your primary anger buttons, is God's design for putting an end to unresolved anger. In fact, I believe that it is actually a spiritual discipline to get angry over the right things and act accordingly.

I want to become a master student of anger
so that I understand where it's coming from
and how to respond in a godly, good way,
rather than a harmful, destructive way.

When the emotion of anger arises within you, *respond to God* rather than *react to people*. What we mean by "respond to God" is that you value all of the trials in your life. You thank God on a daily basis for the irritations and hassles that are unavoidable in relationships, especially in marriage. God gave your mate to you to make you more like Christ. This is one of the true marks of maturity for the follower of Christ, and it's one that I am still learning. I want to become a master student of anger so that I understand where it's coming from and how to respond in a godly, good way, rather than a harmful, destructive way.

The two questions in the next section have been extremely important tools in my awareness of where anger lurks in me. The great thing is that something so brief and memorable could have so much power for change. Let's start with an illustration that is fairly common to us all. Who hasn't struggled with a little "road rage" at times?!

Two Questions That Will Change Your Life (and Marriage) for Good

> **Question 1:**
> *What am I angry about?*

> **Question 2:**
> *What am I going to do with my anger?*

My anger is most quickly displayed while I am driving. We live in a town with a population of 6,000 that hosts 7 million tourists a year. Branson, Missouri, is a family-oriented town, but during certain seasons, we become the senior citizens' capital of the world. And Highway 76, commonly known as "the Strip," is where it can take your car half an hour to move two blocks. During the fall, traffic can be backed up for miles. It's during these times that my wife is thrilled that my license plate does not read "PSTR TED."

As I began to study my anger, I discovered two important questions to ask myself whenever I felt my tension rising. Now when I get into traffic and feel "road rage" creeping up the back of my neck, I ask myself question #1: *What am I angry about?*

There are many reasons why I might be angry, but here are a few:

- That car cut across a double yellow line and in front of me.

- The traffic is causing me to be late to a meeting.

- One of the side roads that serve as a shortcut (that only locals know about) is shut down.

Next, I process these reasons, digging in to what's actually going on behind each one.

That car cut across a double yellow line and in front of me. Behind the reason:

- "That car" is a senior couple driving cautiously because they are new to Branson and don't know their way around, and they just saw the Andy Williams show and are distracted while talking about it.

- "That car" is a young person with no respect for the law or other drivers on the road.

- "That car" is an evil motorist who woke up this morning and said, "I am going to make Ted Cunningham's life miserable today. Can't wait to see him on the road later so I can cut him off. That should do the trick." (This shows you how ridiculous my anger can be at times.)

The traffic is causing me to be late to a meeting. Behind the reason:

- I did not give myself enough time to get there. I should have planned ahead.

- The meeting planners should have scheduled the meeting for 10:30 A.M. instead of 10:00 A.M. so that I would not be late.

- The City of Branson planned a fall festival that they did not tell locals about, which is now causing a spike in traffic. It is their fault I am late. (I don't think I'm alone in my absurdity here. If you are honest, you probably can relate to some of these silly ideas.)

One of the side roads that serve as a shortcut (that only locals know about) is shut down. Behind the reason: This one is definitely the city of Branson's fault.

Once I have a picture of the reasons for my anger, it's time to ask question #2: *What am I going to do about my anger?* Here are my best options:

- Resolve it by taking personal responsibility for my emotions, driving behavior and tardiness.
- Stop playing judge and jury for the infractions of other drivers.

- Plan better next time.

I know this looks and sounds simple, but every time I quiz myself when I feel angry, I always end up feeling a little bit embarrassed as well. When Amy is with me in the car, I often process my anger out loud to her. (Sometimes my wife helps get the process started. When she senses my anger rising toward another driver, she refers to me as "Pastor Ted." Ouch! That's my cue to start processing.)

If I can start by being a student of anger in a situation as common as traffic delays, then I can become a better student of anger in my marriage. I learn how to identify the source of my anger, find a healthy outlet and resolve the situation.

Answering these two questions—"Why am I angry?" and "What am I going to do about my anger?"—is not always easy, and the answers are often anything but black or white. Situations are complicated. Relationships are messy. Yet, I believe that asking these two questions is essential to studying anger and learning how to deal with it.

Your Anger, Your Response: Healthy or Unhealthy?

Consider the following scenarios. For each one, decide if the given response is stuffing it, spewing it or studying it.

DRIVING COMPANIONS

Scenario 1: You're driving down the road and someone stops short ahead of you. Your wife flinches and presses her foot to the floorboard as she grips the dashboard so hard that you wonder if there will be dents in it. You're angry at her apparent distrust of your driving skills, because this is her usual reaction when you drive together. You push down on the horn in frustration as you shoot her a look of irritation. What kind of response are you offering?

A. Stuff it.

B. Spew it.

C. Study it.

Scenario 2: You're driving down the road and someone suddenly cuts you off. In anger, you punch your fist on the horn. You make eye contact with the driver so that the person can see how upset you are. What kind of response are you offering?

    A. Stuff it.
    B. Spew it.
    C. Study it.

DISOBEDIENT CHILD

Scenario 1: You're walking out of the mall, and your five-year-old child begins to run in the parking lot. You call for your child to stop, but she keeps on running. You're mad, but you're extremely concerned. You yell louder in case your child didn't hear you. What kind of response are you offering?

    A. Stuff it.
    B. Spew it.
    C. Study it.

Scenario 2: You're walking out of the mall, and your five-year-old child begins to run in the parking lot. You yell as loud as you can for your child to stop. When she obeys, you proceed to yell at her for running across the lot. Then you give her a spanking on the spot. At a gut level, you know you're spanking your child out of anger and frustration rather than healthy discipline. What kind of response are you offering?

A. Stuff it.

B. Spew it.

C. Study it.

SPOUSE CONFESSES AFFAIR

Scenario 1: Your spouse confesses to an affair. You feel betrayed and angry, but you don't want to lose your spouse. So you go about life pretending like nothing has happened. What kind of response are you offering?

A. Stuff it.

B. Spew it.

C. Study it.

Scenario 2: Your spouse confesses to an affair. You feel betrayed and angry. You decide to let everyone in your spouse's family and work place know through a mass email. What kind of response are you offering?

A. Stuff it.

B. Spew it.

C. Study it.

DELAYED FLIGHT

Scenario 1: Your flight is cancelled due to weather. Unless you can miraculously get on another flight, you're going to miss your spouse's birthday. You can't believe this is happening. You start yelling at the airline personnel. What kind of response are you offering?

A. Stuff it.
B. Spew it.
C. Study it.

Scenario 2: Your flight is cancelled due to weather. Unless you can miraculously get on another flight, you're going to miss your spouse's birthday. You can't believe this is happening. You approach the airline personnel, take a deep breath and calmly let them know the situation to see if they can help. What kind of response are you offering?

A. Stuff it.
B. Spew it.
C. Study it.

HOT GOSSIP

Scenario 1: One of your spouse's family members is slandering you—telling stories about things that you never did and never said. You decide to talk to your spouse about the situation and then launch into a verbal attack about the person who has slandered you. What kind of response are you offering?

A. Stuff it.
B. Spew it.
C. Study it.

Scenario 2: One of your spouse's family members is slandering you—telling stories about things you never did and never said. You take some time before talking with your spouse about the situation, and then do so in a calm manner. What kind of response are you offering?

A. Stuff it.
B. Spew it.
C. Study it.

These two questions are so important because without them it's impossible to follow the instruction of Ephesians 4:26: "In your anger do not sin." In other words, whenever the emotion of anger hits you, you can't allow it to fester overnight. When you ask yourself *What am I angry about?* and *What am I going to do with my anger?* you put yourself in a proactive stance to deal with the anger right away.

Thank God I'm Irritated!

Here is one of the most self-healing insights that I (Gary) have ever learned: Irritation is not in other people or in circumstances I face; all my feelings of irritation reside within me. The same is true of you. I know that's a new way of thinking about the irritations of life, but irritation seems to be God's way of letting us know what areas in our life we need to offer Him to work on.

Often, God uses my irritation with my wife, Norma, to reveal what's really going on inside me. In other words, my irritation with my wife is a sign to show me what I need to work on and to invite me to seek God's healing. As soon as

I take responsibility for my own irritation, the anger directed toward my spouse, other people or circumstances is reduced and I can admit that I still have a long way to go with God before He is finished with me. I've actually begun thanking Him for the privilege of being irritated, because I'm grateful for the chance to track down why I'm irritated and have it work on me so that I can become more like Him in every way.

Let me give you an example. It was 4:00 P.M. on Valentine's Day when I remembered my basketball game. I reached for the phone to call Norma, my bride of less than a year.

"Honey, I forgot to tell you that I have a basketball game tonight. We're supposed to be there about 7:00, so I'll pick you up about 6:30."

Silence hung heavily on the line before she answered, "But this is Valentine's Day."

"Yeah, I know, but I need to be there tonight because I promised the team. I don't want to let them down."

"But I have a special dinner prepared with candles and—"

"Can you hold it off until tomorrow?"

She didn't answer, so I continued (and what I said caused a great deal of damage in our relationship, for like many young husbands, I didn't have the slightest hint how deeply this would wound her): "Honey, you know how important it is for a wife to submit to her husband. I really need to be there tonight, and if we're going to start off with good habits in the early part of our marriage, now is the time to begin. If I'm going to be the leader of the family, I need to make the decisions."

"Ice" perfectly describes the reception I received when I picked her up. It was easy to realize that I had severely offended her, but I figured she had to learn to be submissive sometime, and we might as well start now.

The lifeless expression on her face grew worse as the evening wore on. When we returned home after the game, I noticed that the table was all set up for a special dinner. Candles, our best dishes and pretty napkins were perfectly aligned.

Norma still wasn't speaking to me the next day, so I rushed to the florist to gather several bouquets of flowers, which I put in various spots all over the house. That warmed her up a little. Then I gave her a giant card with a hand on the front that could be turned thumbs-up or thumbs-down.

"Which way is it?" I asked her. She turned it thumbs-up.

I never said whether I was right or wrong, only that I felt badly about the night before. And so began a history of offenses I never knew how to clear up with her. Had someone not shared with me later the secret of developing a lasting and intimate relationship, we might have joined the millions each year who seek divorce.

Couples often ask me, "Where have we gone wrong?" "Why don't we feel romantic toward each other?" "Why do we argue so much?" These problems are not primarily attributable to incompatibility, sexual problems, financial pressure or any other surface issues. They are a direct result of *accumulated offenses*. If a husband and wife can understand how to maintain harmony by immediately working to clear up every hurtful offense between them, they can climb out of such common problems and every marriage's deepest pit: divorce.

Love is not about whether or not I should have gone to the basketball game; love is about recognizing when I hurt my mate's feelings, and then asking how I can repair them.

Letting Go

As you start taking ownership for any anger in your life, you will recognize that if you don't study anger, resolve it and seek forgiveness and restoration, you will rob (and be robbed of) the intimacy you could have with your mate, which God expressly wants you to experience.

Expressing the pain in words and writing down a clear explanation of what happened is important. Even more than that, writing down failures, mistakes and shortcomings can help you on your journey toward personal responsibility and healing.

In the next chapter, we will look deep inside to see what roots of bitterness and unresolved anger may be poisoning your heart. Then you'll have a chance to take the antidote for the poison you have been drinking. We'll also examine the cycle of anger and how you can break out of it.

From GarySmalley.com

Q: *Is "righteous anger" okay? Is it a good thing when I get mad at the sinful behavior of others?*

A: We often like to justify our anger as "righteous indignation," but if we're honest, we have to admit that most of our anger can make no pretense of being righteous. We get angry because we're self-centered. Our anger is a reaction to not receiving what we expected from other people or circumstances. There is nothing righteous about it; it is a blatant assertion of self. Our little ol' finite self is all hacked because we're not getting our way. We believe that life is for our pleasure or excitement. If it's not happening for us, we put our little thumb in our mouth and cry because we can't find our blankie. We kick our legs in the air and scream. And we resolve to keep throwing a tantrum until we get our way.

Sorry to put it so bluntly, but that's exactly what most of our anger really is: a 38-year-old's way of acting like a 4-year-old.

Instead of throwing a tantrum, we may do the adult equivalent of pouting. We've been hurt and we're ready to feel like a victim. Depression, listlessness, isolation and bitterness are on their way, and when we experience these emotions, it's only natural to want to medicate them. It's the human way to ease emotional pain. So we turn to drugs, alcohol, food or anything that makes us feel better. But these "cures" are only momentary. Only one thing can move us toward maturity and health: We must forgive or seek forgiveness. Otherwise, we will slide into the dark, acid pit of unresolved anger.

The Bible says, "Don't sin by letting anger control you. Don't let the sun go down while you are still angry, for anger gives a foothold to the devil" (Eph. 4:26-27, *NLT*). Forgiveness is the valve that allows pent-up anger to vent into oblivion. Forgiveness says, "I know you're not perfect, but neither am I.

So I choose to love you anyway and to forgive you so that I am free to grow in the magnificence of God."

One might feel righteous anger about murder, rape, a cheating spouse or profanity, but even in these cases anger must be resolved. God does not want you or me to hold on to anger forever. We must process our anger with the ultimate goal of resolution. Even God does not hold His anger against us. You and I deserved death because of sin, but He made a way for that anger to be resolved. He resolved His wrath toward us by one name: Jesus.

3

Halt

Breaking the Cycle of Anger

I (Gary) had a heart attack while turkey hunting a few years ago. At the time, my friend and I were in the middle of nowhere without cell service or emergency services. My friend, Junior, had to leave me alone to get the pickup truck. I remember resting my head against a firm bag and looking at the sky. I can still remember the sense of peace that came over me. I prayed, God, I will see You in a couple of minutes. Thank You for my life and my family. I smiled at the thought of my kids and my wife.

I felt like I was dying. My dad and brother had both died from heart attacks, and my older brother had suffered through several major attacks. I knew my time was near.

That's when Junior reappeared. He carried my weak body to the truck and drove into cell-phone range. The paramedics came and I was taken by helicopter to the nearest hospital. On the way, I had enough strength and soundness of mind to call my wife, who was running our ministry at the time. I said, "Hon!"

"Hold on, I've got somebody in here," she answered and put me on hold.

Even as I thought I was going to die, I was irritated. My wife had put me on hold! I told myself, *Fine, I will never talk to her again*—even though I wanted to talk to her more than anything in the whole world for just one last time.

It's amazing to think that even as you're dying, as life is coming to a close, anger can surface so sharply and abruptly. Where does it come from? What are its sources? In the previous chapter, we alluded to those touchy "buttons" that are undetectable until they get pushed. In the upcoming pages, we will explore those buttons—common sources of anger in both men and women that, when pushed, release anger, frustration and even rage. In addition, we will look at the cycle of anger in which many people unknowingly find themselves trapped. We will help you take control of your buttons and make sure they don't get the best of you, your marriage or any other relationship. Finally, we'll uncover some of the hotspots for conflict in your home, workplace and daily life so that you are better prepared to respond with forgiveness and grace.

The Source Beneath the Anger

Most men have an internal button connected to the feeling of being controlled, which provides some insight into the source of a man's anger. They hate to feel powerless.

Ladies, I hate to break this news to you. You may want to sit down. This is something I bet you have never noticed before: *Most husbands do not like to be told what to do.* You can probably do more than imagine the effect this button has on a marriage. You have probably tried, as most wives have, to make suggestions to your husband. In your heart and mind, you were just trying to be helpful—to make things run more efficiently or effectively. But rather than hear the words as a kind suggestion, your husband bristled inside in response. He likely regarded your words as an attempt to control him.

Most men have an internal button connected to the feeling of being controlled. They hate to feel powerless.

Likewise, women have an internal button linked to the feeling of being disconnected in relationships. Most women can't stand rejection and hate being emotionally disconnected. Any time someone withdraws or distances himself during an argument—which is about 80 percent of the time for many men—the woman feels rejected.

Women have an internal button linked to the feeling of being disconnected in relationships. Most women can't stand rejection and hate being emotionally disconnected.

My very favorite button-pushing example from my own life is when my wife and I were in Hawaii for a marriage seminar; we were staying at a downtown hotel right on the beach. One morning, I woke up early, and Norma was still sleeping. I quietly opened the sliding glass door and breathed in the warm salty air. The sun was gently lifting itself from beneath the rugged horizon. The moment was perfect. I was engulfed in the romance of it all. I wanted to be with my wife, my best friend. I wanted to order breakfast on the patio and talk about our marriage goals for the next year. I slipped back into our room and touched her lightly on the shoulder, "Good morning, honey!"

"What?" she said groggily.

"The sun is rising over Diamond Head," I excitedly explained. "Do you want to go out on the balcony and enjoy the sunrise together? Then we could order some food from room service and discuss our marriage goals for the coming year. What do you think?"

"What time is it, Gary?" she asked, crickets still in her voice.

"Six A.M."

"I told you last night before we went to bed that I wanted to sleep until seven," Norma responded. "Don't you remember? We're on vacation."

"Oh, I forgot," I apologized. "But you'll miss the sunrise if you don't come now."

"Seriously, I want to stay in bed for another hour . . . you'll have to enjoy it on your own," she said, rolling away and turning over the pillow to its cooler side.

"No," I protested. "Norma, you're not going to miss this! I'm having a conference here in just a few days, and then we won't have time for this. You can't go back to sleep. Come on."

I grabbed the covers and playfully tugged them away.

"What part of *no* don't you understand?" she asked rhetorically, pulling the sheets back over her.

"Oh, come on," I fearlessly persisted.

I pulled the covers off of her and (in a "gentle" way) grabbed her by the ankles to drag her out of bed. I should have known better—after all, she is my best friend.

Norma didn't like it at all and said something that really hurt my feelings.

I became defensive and zinged her with a comment that really hurt her.

She brought up things from our marriage that had happened years before.

And we were off to the races.

After about an hour, we were still going full speed. Finally, Norma said, "I've had it. You've officially wrecked my day!"

She got out of bed and didn't say another word. I kept talking, trying to engage her, but she just kept moving, and before I knew what had happened, she had left the room fully dressed. I was standing alone in my pajamas.

I looked down at the floor and my bare feet and realized just how alone I really was. I could feel the disconnect in our marriage—which was ironic, because I was scheduled to teach a marriage seminar in just a few days (there's nothing worse than leading a marriage seminar when your wife isn't speaking to you).

I knew that I had to fix things, and fast. I approached Norma when I saw her in the lobby of the hotel in the early afternoon, wanting to see how she was doing. I reached out and took her hand, which she immediately withdrew. I looked around to see if anyone who was registered for the marriage seminar had seen us. I was ready to tell them, "It's okay . . . we'll be better tomorrow!" I was self-conscious about how much disconnect there was in our relationship.

We went our separate ways and crossed paths again in the evening. We were standing near each other when we overheard a woman begin to tell a recently engaged couple about one of my marriage seminar DVDs. The woman was going on and on about how the DVDs had helped her marriage, when Norma put her arm around me. She held me close and placed her chin on my shoulder. Then she whispered, "You ought to order those DVDs."

I'm humbled to say that it took me several days to rebuild the connection with Norma after being so foolish and demanding of her. I placed my own desires over hers—a selfish act—and then pushed her and made her angry with my hurtful comments. I apologized for my self-centeredness and she apologized for her hurtful words, and we were able to make up and reconnect.

Now, why did I get into that big argument with Norma? Because she and I pushed each other's buttons. The argument wasn't really about any particular issue—though you could easily identify some of the surface issues. The real argument was about the deeper buttons we were pushing.

One of Norma's biggest buttons is a fear of failure or of not doing things in the right way. She had 7:00 A.M. in her mind for a leisurely wake-up, and naturally thought I should remember and respect the 7:00 A.M. wake-up request. That's totally fair—except with my personality, everything is negotiable. For me, 7:00 A.M. is a relative thing, like a sign that says "No Parking," but since you only need to be there for a few seconds, of course it's okay to pull in and "park." There's wiggle room. But for Norma, 7:00 A.M. is 7:00 A.M.; and the message of "No Parking" really does mean "No Parking"— even for you! I love that about her; but on that morning in Hawaii, I pushed her button. When I kept asking her to get out of bed, I was inadvertently telling her that she was a failure for not getting up earlier to join me. In addition to feeling (understandably) that I was being rude, she felt her button getting pushed with each persistent thing I said.

I wanted to be Super Husband. In my heart, I wanted to paint a red letter *S* on my chest and dream together about the future and discuss our marriage goals. Is there a more perfect way to start the day? What was I thinking?! I certainly didn't think about Norma—all my thoughts were about *me*.

As we pressed each other's buttons,
the conflict became an angry argument
and escalated out of control.

My wife's reaction to my request took away my super powers. I emotionally read into her response and felt as though she were saying, "My goal this morning is to control Gary and let him know who is boss. If I stay in bed, act stubborn and pretend to be tired, maybe that will make him feel bad about himself."

Was that what she was thinking? Absolutely not. Norma really was tired; she was not trying to upset me. But she inadvertently pushed my *being controlled* and *being belittled* buttons when she corrected me about the wake-up time. She was right, but I took it all wrong. I felt like she was telling me what I could do and when I could do it, and my buttons lit up like a four-alarm fire.

As we continued to press each other's buttons, the conflict became an angry argument and escalated out of control. We spent several days disconnected and several more days reconnecting.

I believe that what we experienced in Hawaii is common to every couple's relationship.

Touching the Main Buttons

Our hot buttons are connected to what we need to feel inside (or believe we need to feel) in order to survive and thrive. For men, those needs can be feeling respected, feeling successful, and so on. For women, those perceived needs relate to feeling secure, loved and connected. Whenever those needs are threatened or outright violated, the button connected to the felt need gets pushed and generates all kinds of emotions that usually result in a feeling of anger or even rage.

Women: Disconnection

Like many women, feeling disconnection in relationships is my wife, Amy's, biggest button. She wants to feel connected to me (Ted), and to family and friends, at all times. I can accidentally push her button by not calling her throughout a day when I'm traveling or by being somewhere else mentally and emotionally when we're together.

Men: Being Controlled

Like many men, feeling like I'm being controlled is my biggest button. I do not like to be told what to do in any way, at any time. Amy can unintentionally push my button by simply handing me a list of things that need to get done (the "honey-do list") or by offering unsolicited advice. When my *being controlled* button is pushed, I can often feel the anger simmering inside, wanting to boil. I have talked with many men who say this is their primary button too.

Has one of these main buttons ever been touched in you? Let's talk a bit more about what the "buttons" are connected to. They are connected to messages that have been written on your heart.

Button Origin and Anger

Where do our buttons come from? Answer: *From lies written on our hearts.* On the following page, we've listed some of the messages written on our hearts.

People have been writing messages on your heart for your entire life. How do these messages affect you? Jesus taught that everything about you flows from your heart (see Luke 6:45), while Solomon wrote that you must guard your heart because that is where life is (see Prov. 4:23). In other words, whatever you think about all day long (meditation)

You'll never amount to anything.

You were a mistake.

Why can't you be more like your brother?!

You're just like your dad.

If you had a brain, you'd be dangerous!

Stupid!

This is how daddy shows his love.

Your mom and I never planned on having you.

I'm leaving your mother.

When will you ever learn?!

If I've told you once, I've told you a thousand times!

eventually seeps into your heart. Once in your heart, all of your words, actions and beliefs flow from there.

We live every single day with the fear that the messages written on our heart may actually be true, and those fears translate directly into buttons. On the following page, we've listed what that looks like.

There are difficulties in every marriage and relationship. You may find yourself in conflict with your spouse over a variety of issues: money, sex, in-laws, parenting, just to name a few. But it's always important to remember that when it comes to anger, the issue is not the issue. The real issue is your fear about what has been falsely written on your heart and those buttons being pressed.

We call this the cycle of anger. Only when you recognize the cycle can you break out of it in your marriage and other

WORTHLESS
You'll never amount to anything.

DEFECTIVE
You were a mistake.

DON'T MEASURE UP
Why can't you be more like
your brother?!

JUDGED
You're just like your dad.

HUMILIATION
If you had a brain, you'd
be dangerous!

SCORNED
Stupid!

DEVALUED
This is how daddy shows his love.

UNWANTED
Your mom and I never planned
on having you.

DISCONNECTION/
REJECTION
I'm leaving your mother.

INFERIORITY
When will you ever learn?!

FAILURE
If I've told you once, I've told
you a thousand times!

relationships. And you will be able to break out of this cycle in the way you respond to the circumstances of your daily life.

The Cycle of Anger

For me (Ted), feeling controlled or belittled are my main buttons. More than anything, I want people to give me respect and free choice. When I don't get them, I can feel my buttons getting pushed. If I don't recognize the cycle's beginning and choose a healthy way to respond, I react by trying to change the person who is pushing my buttons in an attempt to get them to stop. If I can't change them through my words, then I do the second best thing: retreat. I try to run away.

If I feel controlled or judged by something my wife says or does, and I don't think I can change her, my natural (but unhealthy) reaction is to run away. I want to get as far from

the pain as possible. My retreat leads to a sense of disconnection in our relationship, which pushes Amy's buttons of
abandonment and rejection. If she, in turn, chooses an unhealthy reaction to her pain, she pushes my button of failure and further undermines the relationship . . . and the
cycle continues indefinitely.

Here is the portrait, or map, of the cycle of anger in our
marriage:

AMY AND TED'S BUTTONS

When Ted feels . . .
Controlled
Judged
Like a failure
He then . . .

Escalates—raises her word count
Exaggerates-using "always" and "never"
Creates negative beliefs—
assigns motives to actions

Withdraws from the conversation
Defends his opinions
Gets sarcastic

When Amy feels . . .
Disconnected
Abandoned
Rejected
She then . . .

Gary helped me begin to break out of this spin cycle of
anger during that first meeting when I shared with him the
story of my lunch with the associate pastors and that the
church staff had organized a special meeting for the following Sunday to discuss the issues at hand.

"What are you going to do at the meeting?" Gary asked me.

"I will explain and defend myself and try to bring some balance to the drama," I said confidently.

"I wouldn't do that," Gary said. "Instead, you should get up at the end and apologize for everything you have done wrong, and for all your shortcomings."

I couldn't believe Gary's words. They felt like one more blow to an already beat-down, frustrated pastor. Did he really want me to validate what my opponents were saying?

When Amy and I took our places on the front row at the meeting, we were filled with anxiety, fear and anger. We sat and listened for 90 minutes as the staff detailed all of my shortcomings as a leader and pastor to more than 400 people. I firmly held Amy's hand as she choked back tears. It took every last ounce of self-restraint not to jump up and scream, "Knock it off! This is embarrassing to Christ and His Church. This insanity must stop!" But Gary's words haunted me.

Finally, it was my turn to take the microphone. I had a laundry list of defenses I wanted to make. As I looked out across the congregation, I could see the fight in the eyes of church members I had tried to love and nurture and for whom I had prayed on countless occasions. I could remember closed-door conversations with staff members that would embarrass several of my opponents, and part of me longed to spill everything to humiliate them so that they would feel as horrible as I did.

As I stood before the microphone, I took a breath and began one of the longest and most sincere apologies I've ever delivered. I apologized for my failures as a leader, for my retreat-driven behavior and for my brashness in trying to fire a fellow staff member. I apologized for my foolishness, my insecurities and my pride. I promised to do everything I could to work things out, to look for reconciliation in every relationship.

I would like to tell you that the response was warm, compassionate and understanding; but in the end, I was invited to attend a second meeting in two weeks, when the congregation would vote on whether or not to remove me as senior pastor.

During those two weeks, Gary and Michael Smalley kept a close watch on me. They encouraged me to avoid campaigning for my defense and instead trust God. It was one of the hardest things that I've ever done. It was also tough to not withdraw, or become a stuffer, with my wife. If you are a classic withdrawer like me, you know exactly what I mean. When we withdraw from our boss or co-worker, it is hard to come home and be all happy and fun-loving. We only have one heart, and that one heart relates to everyone in our lives. This is why young brides often ask their stuffing husbands, "Are you mad at me?" It is because he is withdrawn, and she just wants to know if she is the source of the withdrawal. Amy knew that she was not the source of my problem, but I had to verbally reassure her nonetheless.

When we walked into that final meeting, Amy leaned over and asked, "How do you want me to vote?" I was wrestling with that question myself.

"Vote your heart," I said.

With more than 300 ballots, it took more than an hour to tally the results. The vote to remove me was unsuccessful by only two votes: mine and Amy's.

I'll never forget that evening. The betrayal . . . the anger . . . the frustration. The disappointment in my board, my church and myself. When we got in the car after the meeting, I was so despondent that I actually turned to Amy and asked how she had voted: Had she betrayed me too? Of course not. But I felt as though the world was against me.

When I shared the story with Gary, he said that it would take two years for me to heal. I did the math: I knew that meant it would take more than 700 sunsets to be fully restored. And it did take that long. However, the journey toward restoration began on that first night when I lay in bed and laid my heart before God and prayed, "Lord, help me to forgive."

Six weeks after the vote, I resigned as senior pastor of the church and moved to Branson, Missouri, where I planted Woodland Hills Community Church. To this day, Gary has only one regret over the whole mess: He still believes that being fired could have been my graduate course in the refining fire of pain. He thinks I was cheated by being voted to stay. (Gary lives and breathes Romans 5:3-5 and James 1:1-4.) In spite of his constant wish for me to experience even greater hardship (or maybe because of it), he has been my mentor ever since that day he helped me take the first steps on my journey to adulthood.

It was through the pain and heartache of those circumstances and relationships that I began to take personal responsibility for everything going on in my life and heart. I began to view every relational interaction, running the gamut from my most personal—my marriage relationship— all the way to the impersonal contacts that are a part of any typical day, as opportunities to study my responses and let God change me. I owe everything that God is now doing with me in ministry to that wonderful church in a small town in southwest Missouri. He used that church to change my life, and I will be forever grateful. (In a later chapter, I share how I reconciled with the founding pastor, who was both my predecessor and successor. Everything truly came full circle.)

Hotspots in Your Marriage

Even if you haven't been (nearly) voted out of a church leadership position, you've undoubtedly faced hotspots—areas of tension—in your marriage, home and workplace. Yet you may not realize just how many potential hotspots there are in relationships!

Especially in marriage, it's important to recognize that men and women are wired differently. If we don't learn to accept and appreciate those differences, then we ignore a potential hotspot, and arguments and anger can erupt.

Especially in marriage, it's important
to recognize that men and women
are wired differently.

Think for a moment about the differences in driving habits of most men and women. Now consider the different housecleaning habits of men and women. Now contemplate the different parenting habits of men and women. Do you see any differences? Do you see any opportunities for conflict? If you don't, look again!

Take, for example, driving-habit differences. Most husbands have heard their wives say, "You're going too fast!" or "Slow down!" or "You're too close to the edge!" Why? Is it because most men secretly want to drive NASCAR? Possibly. But the real reason is that a woman's brain is wired differently from a man's. Most men can judge distances more accurately than most women, particularly at night. If your wife suddenly cries out, "Whoa, you're going to hit that car!" when the car is still a block away, she is demonstrating a fundamental brain difference between men and women.

This difference has affected my (Gary's) marriage. For years, Norma corrected my driving. She was in a major accident during high school and lost several friends. Even today, she is nervous about being on the road. Because of Norma's experiences and the way her brain is wired, I have heard a lot of less-than-encouraging words about my driving—for many years, I felt she was trying to control and belittle me. Eventually, I realized that she wasn't trying to do either; she just wanted to feel safe.

Norma wasn't deliberately pushing my buttons, and slowly I have learned to respond in a healthy way. Now when she corrects my driving (which I definitely need from time to time), I follow the advice of James 1:19 and am quick to listen and slow to speak. I respond by blessing her with the simple words, "Thank you, honey," even when she asks me to slow down and I don't really want to. But I do want to help her feel safe. I've realized that God is using my wife to help me come to terms with my own buttons, and to mature.

Hotspots at Work

Hotspots at work are important to recognize because they often follow us home. I (Gary) work with my son, Michael, which can be both challenging and incredibly rewarding. We were recently in Dallas, Texas, to share on a morning show the news of one of our most successful marriage programs for people who are near to getting divorced. My son and I told the whole country how to live in harmony, discover peace and bring the love back into their homes.

After the 45-minute interview, we decided to stop at a Barnes & Noble bookstore on our way to the next interview. I was chattering away, while Michael didn't say a word.

"Hey, you're not talking . . . what's wrong?" I asked.

"Nothing," he responded coldly.

"Something's wrong. I mean, you always talk. What's up?"

"Sure, I'll talk," Michael said harshly. "I'm not ever going on TV with you again. You're going on this next one alone."

I heard his words, but what was harder to hear was his tone, which sounded belittling and controlling to me. "What's your problem?" I asked angrily.

"You interrupted me continually on that show," he said. "I had a really good concluding point to make and you in-terrupted me."

Not acknowledging the seriousness of the situation, I quipped, "Well, if you had anything important to say, I wouldn't interrupt you." I had no idea how much those words would hurt my son. I still wish I could take them back. "And besides, you're just as bad about interrupting me," I added.

Michael reacted to the pain with anger and defensiveness: "I never interrupt you!"

"Let's get a copy of the tape and see how many times you interrupted me," I said.

The argument escalated and continued for more than 30 minutes. We had just finished an interview on a morning show, talking about harmony, peace and love, and now we were out of control! We were like two scrappy elementary school kids on a playground, fighting for all we were worth.

Somewhere in the midst of the heated argument, I realized the issue wasn't really about the television show or interruptions. It was about our buttons. I took a breath and said firmly but gently, "You know, here's the bottom line: I've been on television a lot longer than you. If I sense that what you're saying is losing the audience, and they're flicking through one of the other 500 channels they can go to, I am going to say something to keep the crowd."

Those words reminded us that we were on the same team. Michael relaxed, leaned back in the chair and extended his right hand: "Give me five!"

I gave him five.

"Dad, that's amazing," he said. "I interrupt you for the exact same reason. I think you're old, out of date and irrelevant.

I think I have sharper, newer ideas and I want to bring those in to snag the audience, so I cut you off."

"That *is* funny. Give me five," I said.

Then Michael and I talked about what we had been doing to each other for the last half-hour: pushing each other's buttons.

Michael's primary button is rejection. What had I done on the morning show? I had rejected his thoughts and ideas by interrupting him. Interruption is rejection. What had Michael done to me afterward? He had belittled me and made me feel controlled when he said I had to do the next show without him. I reacted poorly to my buttons being pushed by pushing harder on his button of rejection . . . and the cycle was set in motion.

If we had not taken the time to neutralize the anger, it would have continued to build. Eventually I would have taken the anger home with me and shared my frustration with Norma. Likewise, whether you realize it or not, your hotspots at work follow you home and affect your marriage. When irritations at work begin to make you angry, you *will* find an outlet. And spewing on your mate is not a healthy way to grow a marriage.

---

*The good news is that it only takes one person
to stop the whole cycle of anger. One person can
do it, and that person is you!*

The good news is that it only takes one person to stop the whole cycle of anger. One person can do it, and that person is you! The other person doesn't have to change. Just you. When you stop pushing the other person's button, you naturally take away the fuel from the fire of contention.

Hotspots in Other Relationships

I have a good friend named Dan who works at my bank. Dan and I meet regularly to talk about various investments—at least once a month, simply because I can't remember anything financial for more than a few weeks. He provides a printout so that I can see how things are going.

One month, Dan and I were reviewing the financial information and discovered a small savings account in Phoenix that had remained inactive since Norma and I had moved away from Arizona years ago.

"What do you want to do with it?" Dan asked.

"Let's have everything in one place," I responded confidently. "Take it out of there. I don't want it."

I signed a legal document and Dan proceeded to close the account as instructed. I never thought about it again.

A month or so later, Norma (who has a button called "doing things right") said, "Gary, someone has stolen all our money from Phoenix. They've taken my savings account."

"Really?" I said. "Show me the papers."

Completely forgetting my financial meeting of the previous month, I called the bank in Phoenix and said, "Someone has stolen the money from our account! We need to find out what happened right away."

The banker explained that someone named Dan had emptied the account.

I couldn't believe what the banker was telling me. *Why would Dan do that? Why would my friend empty my wife's savings account?*

I made a beeline for the bank. "Dan, we have a serious problem here," I said. "The bank in Phoenix says that you drew out Norma's savings."

"I did," he answered. "Gary, you told me to do that."

"I would have never instructed you to take my wife's savings out of Phoenix," I protested.

"We met about a month ago and you told me to empty it!" Dan said.

"That's it! You're in trouble," I responded. "I've been investigating who did this and it says right here that it was you. You'll have to explain this to Norma."

I stormed out of the bank, frustrated and angry.

By the time I got home, Dan had called Norma and explained the whole situation. And in the end, it was me—not Dan—who was in trouble.

In one foolish interaction, I managed to push two people's buttons. I pushed Norma's buttons by taking control of her money and not doing things the right way (which cost us some bank fees and interest). I pushed Dan's button by belittling and trying to control him—the very buttons I struggle with.

Notice, however, that though I pushed Dan's and Norma's buttons, they didn't push back. Dan maintained his composure with a gentle but firm response to me. And while Norma still teases me about the mishap, she never allowed her frustration to escalate. She didn't push my buttons in response.

In every relationship, you can diffuse conflict by simply resisting the urge to push the other person's buttons, even when he or she pushes yours. As demonstrated by Dan and Norma, when you take responsibility for your emotions, words and actions, you can avoid pushing people's buttons and escalating a situation. When you do, you will feel empowered and connected in your relationships, and that will affect your marriage for the better.

In the next chapter, we will examine the importance of taking responsibility for your emotions—especially anger—and offer some ways to help you deal with it. In addition, we will expose three of the most common expressions of anger. Even if you don't describe yourself as a person with "anger issues," you may be surprised to discover what's lurking just below the surface of your reactions and behavior.

From GarySmalley.com

Q: *I am engaged to be married in two months, and the devil has attacked my relationship with words, resentment and division. I know I love this man, who is a strong Christian, but how do we stop all this bickering? I cannot believe the things we've spoken to each other these last few days. Please help.*

A: Let me answer your question with a question. Is the devil attacking your relationship with words, resentment and division, or are you and your spouse attacking each other? James 4:1 pinpoints the source of conflict: "What is causing the quarrels and fights among you? Isn't it the whole army of evil desires at war within you?" (*NLT*).

We all have the same choice to make, a choice that will largely determine whether we enjoy deep, satisfying relationships or deal with fragile, disappointing ones. I can't stress enough how crucial it is that both you and your fiancé take personal responsibility for your actions and emotions.

4

Own

Taking Responsibility

When I (Gary) was a kid, a friend and I were running around in the woods behind the Smalley home. We weren't paying attention to where we were going and ran right into the middle of a rattlesnake den. We froze when we heard the symphony of rattles. I remember being paralyzed by fear, but my friend managed to grab a nearby branch and move one of the rattlers out of the way. I grabbed a branch and followed suit. As soon as we cleared a path, we ran away as hard and as fast as we could.

I've never forgotten that terrifying day. I still wonder how we could have gotten into a rattlesnake den at all! I have no idea.

But the real wonder was our getting out.

Everyone steps into a rattlesnake den of anger from time to time. You may be running hard and fast in life, and then suddenly you look around and see deadly venom all around you. You're not sure how you got there, but that's not the most important question. The crucial problem is getting out.

Walking Toward a Snake Den

Gary has served as my mentor for the past seven years, and I (Ted) heed his advice and counsel in every area of my life. I can honestly say there is not an issue of theology, ministry, leadership or family that I have fought him over. There is only one strong disagreement we have ever had, and it led to one of the worst vacations of my life.

In the summer of 2005, Gary talked me into getting a camper for my family. He told me it would be the best thing that ever happened to us.

Instead, that camper was the source of one of our worst vacations, our biggest marital fights and our closest near-death experience.

After purchasing the camper, we planned a two-week trip through Colorado. Unfortunately, the same month we made the purchase, the price of gasoline rose more than a dollar a gallon. We said good-bye to the Rockies and decided to stay closer to home.

Our first attempt to park was an introduction to the frustration and anger we were to face during the entire trip. Backing the camper onto the narrow camping slab proved to be quite a challenge. Amy stood about 15 feet off of the back bumper, which meant she was about 50 feet away from me. While motioning me into the spot, she started yelling, "Whoa, whoa, whoa, a little more to the left!"

That was only the beginning of our struggles, irritations and conflict.

On day two, Amy and I tried to take down the awning in a 50-mph windstorm. Had it not been for seasoned campers on the next site, I'm sure our camper would have turned into a sailing vessel and flipped upside down.

By day three, Amy and I had discovered that we didn't really care for the activities involved in the camping experience. You can only eat so many s'mores, sit around in lawn chairs for so many hours and burn so much food over a campfire. We were bored.

By day four, Amy admitted, "We should have researched this trip a little more."

"Hey, we only have 10 days left, so let's make the most of it!" I said, in an attempt to be the eternal optimist. And then it hit me: *I had become my parents.* We were going to have fun *no matter what.*

By day seven, Amy and I realized that camping was making us tired and irritable. We weren't sleeping well and we weren't having fun. I calculated the cost of our RV vacation, including the down payment, supplies, campground fees and high fuel costs, and I realized we could have spent a week in Hawaii instead of two weeks camping in Arkansas . . . but I still wasn't ready to head home and give up.

We decided to try one more campsite.

By the time we got set up, I knew that I needed a time-out. I decided to go to Wal-Mart by myself for supplies. During my shopping venture, I spent a little time alone with the Lord in prayer. I wanted to take responsibility for my attitudes and frustrations. I realized that I had forced Amy into this trip and it was my fault. She always supported my whims and dreams, even when they stretched the limits of her comfort zone. I needed to humble myself and apologize. I needed to take responsibility.

On the drive back to the camper, I worked out my apology in my head. But when I pulled up to the campsite, I heard an unfamiliar beeping sound. When I opened the camper door, I immediately recognized it: the propane was on.

While I was gone, Amy had accidentally brushed the knob on the stove, which turned on the propane without a fire and turned our camper into a giant propane tank. If there had been just one spark . . .

Amy was taking a nap. I grabbed her and the baby and pulled them outside. When Amy woke up, she had a tremendous headache from inhaling the gas but was otherwise okay. I was so grateful that my family was safe! I hugged them tightly as the camper aired out, and then began packing up to head home.

The camper sold a few months later. We have never looked back.

Here is what I learned: Life's little irritations, left unchecked, can grow into major frustrations and become dangerous to our health and safety. To keep anger at bay, even the most minor irritations need to be dealt with. Anger does not happen overnight. It appears when the negligible has been neglected.

Expose and resolve life's irritations and frustrations at the seed level. Do not water or fertilize them with time, emotional energy or pride. Do not let them take root. Let them fall on dry ground and recognize when it's time to run in the opposite direction.

How to Be a Good Snake Handler

Just last night I had a button pushed. I was offended. Worse, I wanted to lash out; but by God's grace, I avoided the rattlesnake den. In this chapter, you'll discover five tactics for climbing out of the den of anger. You don't have to live there even one more day! You can break out of any cycle of anger you're in.

Tactic 1: Call a Time-out

My typical reaction when Amy and I fight is withdrawal. Fight or flight? My instinct is flight, every time. I shut down my heart. I physically remove myself and go into another room. I don't want to talk to her. I don't want to look at her.

I don't want to take responsibility. Without realizing it, I'm snuggling up with the deadly snakes of anger.

A time-out is designed to help you and your spouse find a solution and move toward resolution.

A far better tactic is to call a time-out. Withdrawal and time-outs are both a form of retreat, but a time-out is designed to help you and your spouse discover a solution and move toward resolution. When used correctly, a time-out leads to reconnection and communication, because it quenches the flames of a flared temper and requires you to take responsibility for your attitudes and emotions.

James 1:19 instructs, "My dear brothers, take note of this: Everyone should be quick to listen [and] slow to speak." Being quick to listen means listening until you understand what is happening and why it's happening; yet many couples are quick to speak and slow to listen. Time-outs give both spouses time to get out of the snakes' den before they make things worse.

It's a good idea to lay some healthy ground rules for your time-out. Establish a set amount of time to cool down so that you aren't away from each other for an indefinite amount of time. Before you leave for the time-out, take a few moments to regain your composure. Check your voice. Is it calm? Check your body language. Are your arms crossed? Do you appear withdrawn, or does your body communicate that you want to remain connected? Verbally acknowledge that you and your spouse are on the same team and that you both want to find resolution and understanding.

Tactic 2: Cry Out to God

When you're facing a pit of angry rattlesnakes, it's a great time to pray! Ask God for His wisdom and His resolution of the situation. Ask Him to give you a humble heart and the right attitude to talk with your spouse. Ask Him to help you see your spouse's side of the argument. And ask Him to keep you humble. The Bible says, "God opposes the proud but gives grace to the humble" (Jas. 4:6). The word "grace" here does not refer to the grace of salvation. The word in this context means "enabling power." In other words, God empowers the humble to do His will.

All too often, when tempers flare, we are tempted to retreat. We lick our wounds and try to figure out how to make the pain stop—apart from God's wisdom or grace. Retreating without prayer is an expression of pride, whereas depending on God and admitting that *we* are the problem expresses humility. An attitude of humility is demonstrated when we ask God how to change and what to do differently. We demonstrate humility when we ask God to expose our sin and pride. We express humility when we ask God to reveal the areas where He wants us to grow. Through prayer, we can take responsibility for what's going on inside our heart.

Humility asks God how we can change
and what we can do differently.

When you're faced with a conflict, the first person to call out to is God—not your family or friends. When I conduct a wedding, I usually ask, "Who gives this woman to be married to this man?" I literally mean *give*. Sometimes a mom comes up to me and says, "I don't feel like I'm losing my daughter today; I feel like I'm gaining a son."

I am always quick to say, "No, you're losing a daughter."

Don't turn to your mom, dad, sister, brother or best friend to find an ally. You will not always find the best counsel from others. Instead, turn to God. The Bible tells us we can ask God for wisdom and He will give it. He gives His grace to the humble who admit their helplessness before Him.

Get Grafted!

Jesus instructs us in John 15:1-5:

> I am the true vine, and my Father is the gardener. He cuts off every branch in me that bears no fruit, while every branch that does bear fruit he prunes so that it will be even more fruitful. You are already clean because of the word I have spoken to you. Remain in me, and I will remain in you. No branch can bear fruit by itself; it must remain in the vine. Neither can you bear fruit unless you remain in me.
>
> I am the vine; you are the branches. If a man remains in me and I in him, he will bear much fruit; apart from me you can do nothing.

This passage is a beautiful description of what God desires to do in and through you. Jesus is the Vine; you are a branch of the Vine. When you connect to Christ, God's only vine here on Earth, He sends His Holy Spirit to "drip" the living sap into your veins. All you have to do to receive it is cry out to Him, get connected and then rest in Him. When you, as a branch, are well connected to Jesus, the Vine, you will begin to catch yourself acting like God does.

You'll also experience a need for God's Word to be hidden in your heart. That's one of the main ways His "sap" enters your veins. As you meditate on His commands to love Him and love others, He transforms you through His Word.

Everyone who is in Christ comes to new life. If you are ready to connect to His life, you can follow these steps in prayer:

1. I confess (admit) to You, God, that I have been connected to all of the wrong things—parents, society's beliefs and ways, friends and other influences—up until today. I confess that I only want Your beliefs to control me and I only want You to be my God. I want to be grafted onto the True Vine, Jesus, and abide in Him from now on.

2. I repent by cutting "self" off right now. I feel myself falling to the ground.

3. By Your grace, lift me up and carry me to the Vine, because I am weak, helpless and "poor in spirit." Only You, God, can connect me to the Vine. Use Your "sap" to seal me for eternity, having given Your life-blood to make me a part of Your family.

4. With Your power, God, running through my veins, I will hide Your Word in my heart. I will graft Your words on my heart so that I begin to think, speak and act like You. I don't live here anymore. My new life is hidden in You by faith, and the life that I now live, I live by the Son of God who loves me and gave Himself for me. Let Your life and love pour out of me to others.

Tactic 3: Commit to Forgiving Your Mate

There are two word pictures that are helpful when thinking about forgiveness. The first is untying knots. The second is erasing the offense.

When you refuse to resolve relationship issues, knots and tangles of resentment and bitterness bind your subconscious mind. They ensnare you and tie you up—and when you're ensnared, you can't enjoy the freedom and joy God desires to give you. When you choose to forgive, on the other hand, you untie the knots put into a relationship by letting go of the offense. And the moment you forgive someone, God unties your own tangles. He frees your heart and releases His grace and power to love others.

To use another word picture: Forgiveness is erasing the offending incident from the relationship's story. Forgiveness means going to the marker board and completely wiping away all the wrongs done to you. Whatever your mate did is gone. The board is blank. The issue is not there anymore. The offending mate is released from the guilt he or she has been carrying, and the offended mate is relieved of all the baggage of bitterness, resentment and anger that has been weighing him or her down. As the Bible instructs, "Get rid of all bitterness, rage, anger, harsh words and slander, as well as all types of malicious behavior. Instead, be kind to each other, tenderhearted, forgiving one another just as God, through Christ, has forgiven you" (Eph. 4:31-32).

Marriage and other relationships do not work unless you create an atmosphere of forgiveness. You may be tempted to say, "What my husband (wife) did to me is unforgivable," but before you do, remember all that God has forgiven you. Show me an unforgiving person, and I will show you someone who does not understand all they have done against Christ. Show me an unforgiving person, and I will show you someone oblivious of the fact that he or she is standing in a rattlesnake pit. That person is clueless. He doesn't realize that Christ died so that he doesn't have to live in the snake pit.

Cultivate an atmosphere of forgiveness in your marriage, and it will impact every aspect of your life. We will discuss more about how to embrace a forgiving spirit in chapter 6.

Tactic 4: Choose a Different Reaction

Do you have scripts in your marriage? Scripts are arguments that are repeated again and again. Whether you realize it or not, you've probably been using some scripts in your marriage for years. Here are a few "script" examples:

- "I don't want to talk about it right now."
- "You never want to talk about it."
- "You make me so mad."
- "You never think about me or my feelings."
- "I am the husband/leader; I get the final say."
- "You shouldn't feel that way."
- "That's a crazy way to feel."

If you recognize any of these statements, you need to develop a different reaction. Why? Because it's one thing to stumble into a rattlesnake den and it's another thing to make the pit your play area. The Bible describes a foolish man as one who looks in a mirror and "after looking at himself . . . goes away and immediately forgets what he looks like" (Jas. 1:24). Have you taken a good look at yourself lately? At your reactions? At your responses? Is it possible that the common denominator in your anger issues is you?

You can "flip the script" by responding to God rather than to the person in front of you. You can take ownership of your attitudes and reactions.

When you are in a conflict or a heated discussion, your heart screams the loudest. Out of the mouth, the heart speaks.

I love it when people say things like, "Let me tell you what's on my heart" or "I have searched my heart on this." We call this "the Halo Complex." Jesus was referring to the Halo Complex in His log-and-speck illustration recorded in the Bible in Matthew 7. Have you ever considered that you never need to explain to people what is going on in your heart? You may think that's crazy, but it's true: Your words and reactions speak loud and clear about what is going on in your heart; and when you are in a conflict or a heated discussion, your heart screams the loudest. Out of the mouth, the heart speaks.

How do most men look at themselves in the mirror? They look fast. How long do most women spend looking in the mirror? They spend a long time. Many people approach the Bible as a man approaches a mirror. They just glance inside like a man glances in the mirror, and then they are gone. Yet if you spend time in the Scriptures, you not only discover who you are, but you also discover who you are created to be.

You may be having the same fights in your marriage, your workplace and in various other relationships without even realizing it. Take a step back and take a good long look at yourself in the light of Scripture. The Bible says, "The man who looks intently into the perfect law that gives freedom, and continues to do this, not forgetting what he has heard but doing it—he will be blessed in what he does" (Jas. 1:25). In other words, if you examine your heart, actions and reactions before God, you are likely to see the need for change and growth. Simply choosing a different reaction will break habits that have been developed over years.

For me (Ted), this means staying in the room and discussing the problem with my wife when my heart is screaming, "Get out! You'll be safer!" For you, it may mean closing your mouth when your heart and voice are screaming. It may mean making eye contact with your spouse when you want to look away. It may mean avoiding humor and sarcasm and instead taking the moment seriously.

Tactic 5: Create Judgment-Free Zones

Without even realizing it, many couples fall into something we like to call "the Dance of the Lumberjacks," which focuses on what your spouse is doing wrong. Jesus gave us the key for putting an end to the Dance of the Lumberjacks when He taught, "First take the plank out of your own eye then you will see clearly to remove the speck from your brother's eye" (Matt. 7:5).

The words "plank" and "log" are synonyms. The idea is that one spouse walks around with a big log of wrongdoing sticking out of his eye—but he can only see the tiny speck of sawdust (albeit wrongdoing) in his mate's eye (or vice versa!). Round and round they go. The finger-pointing dance keeps repeating.

How do you stop the dance? The only way is to create judgment-free zones. You simply forget the speck of sawdust in your mate's eye and recognize the presence of a big log in your own. (Judgment-free zones can only exist when we remove the roadblocks to forgiveness, which we will show you how to do in chapter 8.)

Security comes from knowing that
your mate loves you in spite of your
flaws and shortcomings.

Looking at the log in your own eye before removing the speck from your mate's is highly critical to the wellbeing of your marriage. The reason is quite simple: Judgment destroys security. The mate who is always having his or her eyes examined for specks has a sense of being under constant scrutiny. He or she feels pressured to measure up in order to keep the love of the other. The message is, "If you want me to continue loving you, you'd better get rid of that irritating habit." This does not express unconditional love, and it's hardly the way to create security in a marriage. Security comes from knowing that your mate loves you in spite of your flaws and shortcomings. Real love is unconditional.

That's why judgment-free zones are so important. They allow your spouse to be all that God created him or her to be. In a judgment-free zone, your spouse can share all of her deepest insecurities. He can share his deepest fears and doubts. He or she can share without fear of being rejected, abandoned or mocked. Judgment-free zones are one of the hallmarks of a secure marriage.

Three Expressions of Anger

Anger will always find a way to express itself. Like the lead in a play, anger will get plenty of stage time in your life. The question is, which act of the play are you in?

Act One: Repay It

I (Ted) can think of lots of examples of how I repay it while driving. I am constantly teaching people with my car. Just a couple of years ago, Amy and I were returning from a trip, and I was tired. We landed in the Springfield Airport, and Amy went to baggage claim while I went to get the car.

Our airport is a small regional facility and is easy to get around—there's just one loop for driving and one terminal for airplanes. As I got on the loop to return to the terminal, a 40-ish man cut me off pulling into the turn lane, nearly missing my front bumper. (When I say "nearly," I mean by inches, not feet.) Instead of honking and then proceeding to curbside where Amy was waiting with our luggage, I pulled in behind the man and hurried the bags and Amy into the car, because I was going to beat him out of the airport. (Did I mention the fact that I was very tired? It is not an excuse, but I am hoping you'll cut me a little slack.)

Exiting the airport, the guy and I were neck and neck. I had one advantage: This was *my* airport. I had already taken notice of the little green sticker in the lower left corner of his car's trunk that indicated it was a rental. He had no clue that at the exit, the left lane is forced to reenter the terminal. Armed with this knowledge, I stuck right by his side. If it was the last thing I did, I was going to teach this guy a lesson.

As the exit approached, Amy asked, "Are you going to let that guy in?" There's only one right answer to that question. You know it and I know it. But deep down I was thinking, *He cut me off. This is my one chance to come out on top and be victorious! I must win.*

Our entire town's economy is based on the 7 to 8 million tourists that visit our community each year. If the local pastors treat people this way, it's hard to imagine how we have been successful. Silly, right? Here I am, Pastor Ted, just returned from a trip where I was encouraging couples with the love of Jesus.

I am thrilled to report that I answered Amy's question in the affirmative. Though it pained me, I let the other guy win.

We're all tempted to repay hurts and offenses with anger from time to time, but the Bible challenges us to resist the temptation. In Romans 12:19, Paul writes, "Do not take revenge, my friends, but leave room for God's wrath, for it is written: 'It is mine to avenge; I will repay,' says the Lord."

Okay, be honest. Do you tend to want to repay hurts or offenses connected to your spouse's words or behavior? Are you remembering something right now about which you would like to get back at your spouse? The desire for revenge is a heavy weight to carry, isn't it? If you would like to permanently unburden yourself from the weight of constantly looking for ways to repay offenses, then your first decision is to decide not to take revenge. Revenge in word or deed is not an option anymore. Once you make that decision, here are guidelines for resolving your anger and reconciling your relationship with your spouse, if needed:

1. *Start on the basis of acceptance.* Let your husband (wife) know that the issue can be resolved. You love and care for him, even though there has been a disagreement.

2. *Settle the issue of blame.* Do not go to your spouse with an accusatory attitude; that will put a quick end to your efforts at reconciliation. People do not warm up to accusation. Accusation pours more fuel on the fire. Let your spouse know that the question of fault no longer matters, but the relationship does.

3. *Share your enthusiasm.* What?! Explain how you have grown from this experience and that you

know there is still more to learn. Show your enthusiasm about being a great learner, not a "relationship expert."

4. *Save room for growth.* The best attitude is "I am not perfect. I need to grow." Find something to apologize for. Don't make something up— if you look hard enough, you can find something! It may be as simple and serious as snubbing each other, giving each other the silent treatment, gossiping with a friend about the offense or harboring negative beliefs about the motives of your spouse.

The four-step process of retraining your thoughts begins with *acceptance* of the other person, and then is characterized by *no blame*, by *thankfulness* for lessons learned and by a humble *apology* for your own part of the disagreement.

Notice the phrase "if it is possible" in the passage above. You may be in a situation in which the person you're angry with is no longer living or is no longer in your life. It's not possible for you to reconcile with that person because he or she is gone. Here are a few ideas for handling situations when it is no longer possible to have a one-on-one conversation:

1. *Write a letter and have a loved one read it aloud.* Hearing words of healing and forgiveness can be a great release.

2. *Have a conversation with the person.* Talking to yourself is not always a bad thing. Picture the

person in the room and say what you were never able to say to them while they were living. This is a version of the therapist's method of "empty-chair counseling."

3. *Ask the Lord to release the anger.* Pray for the person by name. Describe the event in detail. The more you hold back, the more unresolved anger you will hold on to.

As followers of Jesus, we are not to take revenge. In fact, we are to hope that the person will get off the hook and we are to look for ways to live at peace with them.

When we react in anger to what someone has said or done, a common temptation is to repay them with the same pain they have caused us. Yet according to the Romans 12 passage, as followers of Jesus, we are not to take revenge. In fact, we are to hope that the person will get off the hook and we are to look for ways to live at peace with them. Ultimately, God is the one who will repay—not us. It's so important to let God be God. Let Him take care of His people. Let Him take care of the situation. If your spouse is imperfect, it's not your job to preach or teach or change him (or her). It's God's job.

Whenever you find yourself trying to repay, you're caught in Act One. You're trying to play God. But only one person is in the heart-changing business, and that is Jesus Christ. First Peter 3:9 instructs, "Do not repay evil with evil or insult with insult, but with blessing, because to this you were called so that you may inherit a blessing." Leave room for God to take the lead in every situation and relationship. Instead of reacting to people, respond to God.

Act Two: Replay It

Do you rehearse some of your recurring arguments in your head? Do you ever find that you're kicking yourself about what you *should* have said to your spouse? Do you find yourself replaying an argument again and again?

Replaying anger is like gossip: We tend to make up details that didn't actually happen, and by doing so, we can even begin to develop negative beliefs. Replaying anger is also similar to studying the Bible poorly. There are two common mistakes we make when studying the Bible. One, we don't see enough. We overlook details about the text and miss some great nuggets. Two, we see too much, things that are not there. When we rehearse the scripts of fights in our head, we have a tendency to overlook important details and see things that are not there.

We were having a meeting one morning among our pastoral staff around a Starbucks coffee table. We were planning the next year's sermon series when John turned to me and said, "What can we offer on Sunday mornings for people who want to go deeper?"

I had no idea that one single question could push so many buttons at once! Here are just a few of the things my heart heard in his question:

- "Ted, you are shallow."
- "You do not take the Bible seriously enough."
- "You're full of fluff."
- "Expository preaching rules—all other styles drool."
- "Woodland Hills is heading down the wrong road."
- "I (John) am the all-knowing possessor of great truth and wisdom."
- "I am not following your leadership."

John did not say any of that, but those negative beliefs are where my heart took his simple question. I ran with a ball that John never threw onto the field.

He did not see all my thoughts, but he did see my reactions. I take full ownership of my foolishness that day. I reacted to everything he had (and hadn't) said by doing everything I didn't want him to do. (We call that "the mirror principle." What bugs us in others is probably something we struggle with ourselves.)

I apologized later for my actions that day at Starbucks and John reciprocated, but for a week after that morning, things were pretty touch and go.

Although this scenario is not from marriage, it certainly has the earmark of the kinds of thoughts that can grow from almost nothing when a husband or wife is a replayer. It's so easy to read into a simple comment and start a full-scale disagreement, isn't it? But we must stop increasing the size of the "offense" based on the sensitivity of our buttons. Those sensitive buttons *will* get pushed. So we must own our emotions and let God be God.

Are You a Replayer?

Take this quick quiz to see if you are a replayer. Circle the number, 1 to 5, that best describes you.

1. **I talk to myself.**
   I do this all the time.   5 4 3 2 1   I don't do this at all.

2. **I argue with my spouse in my head.**
   I do this all the time.   5 4 3 2 1   I don't do this at all.

3. **I add statements that were never made to past conversations.**
   I do this all the time.   5 4 3 2 1   I don't do this at all.

4. **I end closeness with my spouse based on single conversations.**
   I do this all the time.   5 4 3 2 1   I don't do this at all.

5. **I can remember details from conversations that happened years ago.**
   I do this all the time.   5 4 3 2 1   I don't do this at all.

6. For a long time afterward, when I talk with my spouse, my mind immediately returns to a particular conversation that made me angry.
I do this all the time. 5 4 3 2 1 I don't do this at all.

7. I lose sleep over our conversations from the past.
I do this all the time. 5 4 3 2 1 I don't do this at all.

8. I find myself venting about my anger more than once to someone during a single conversation.
I do this all the time. 5 4 3 2 1 I don't do this at all.

9. I find myself venting over an issue to as many people who will listen to me.
I do this all the time. 5 4 3 2 1 I don't do this at all.

10. I have often thought, *Here is what I will say the next time.*
I do this all the time. 5 4 3 2 1 I don't do this at all.

Add up the total: _____

If you scored 25 or under, you're tempted to replay an issue from time to time but you also know how to let it go. Continue turning to God each time you think about replaying an issue and allow Him to still your heart.

If you scored 25 or higher, you tend to replay issues in your mind. Replaying can undermine all of your relationships—especially your marriage. Instead of replaying an issue, look for resolution. Spend time in prayer with God and engage in honest, grace-filled conversation with your spouse as soon as possible.

You know you're in Act Two when you're lying in bed at night rehearsing the same situation. You start going over it, and before you know it, you look at the clock and an hour has gone by. You're tossing and turning, staring at the ceiling, hoping to make it stop. You can't. A second hour passes. Sometime between the third and fourth hour, you finally fall asleep, but when you wake up, the situation is the first thing on your mind.

In Philippians 4:8, Paul gives instructions for what to focus our minds on: "Finally, brothers, whatever is true, whatever is noble, whatever is right, whatever is pure, whatever is lovely, whatever is admirable—if anything is excellent or praiseworthy—think about such things."

If you study this verse, you'll notice there are eight things (go ahead, count 'em) that the Scripture invites us to focus our attention on. Why? Because what you rehearse or replay in your mind will eventually seep into your heart as a belief. If you constantly tell yourself that you didn't handle things well, you failed or you're worthless, you will begin to believe it. And if you repeatedly tell yourself that someone else failed or is worthless, you will begin to believe it, which makes forgiveness and reconciliation all the more difficult.

You may be like me and have a tendency to replay conversations years after the fact. What is the one thing you and I can do about that? Hit the Stop button. Stop rewinding. Choose to no longer go back and make up details or events that never happened or were never intended.

Instead of replaying what went wrong or what is wrong in your life, begin following the advice of Paul. Refocus your

Own: Taking Responsibility

thinking on the good things. Look for reasons not just to live, but to be fully alive. Focus on the truths that you are a child of God, that He loves you and that He cares for you deeply. Reflect on Psalm 139, which says that God's caring thoughts toward you are innumerable. When that becomes the focus of your day, you jam the tape that replays the same situation that results in the same harmful thoughts over and over again. And when you stop replaying the same situation, you are in a position to move forward in your life and all that God has for you in the way of abundant living. When we turn the universe back over to God, it is amazing how well we can sleep.

If you repay it or replay it, you won't be able to move on to Act Three—the one that will change your life, your marriage and all your relationships.

Act Three: Resolve It

A few months ago, our daughter, Corynn, was outside playing in the evening.

All of her friends in the neighborhood are older, and she has the earliest bedtime. I called for her to come home and take a bath before bed.

"I don't want to take a bath," she answered, her little arms crossed firmly.

Like most parents, I started to say, "Corynn, I'm only going to say this four more times," but before I could finish the sentence, I noticed our neighbor Jean watching our interaction.

"Corynn, I need you in here right now," I finished calmly with a smile.

She walked in the house and she was mad. She was only five, but I could tell she was wrestling with her temper.

"It's time for a bath—let's go!"

"No!" she said defiantly.

"Enough, it's time for a bath and bed!"

Then Corynn said: "I hate you and Mommy."

Those words stung my soul, but I took a deep breath and knelt down to her height. "Do you know what the word 'hate' really means?" I asked.

"No," she said sheepishly.

"I need you to go get my Bible," I said.

After a few moments, she returned with my Bible. "I want to teach you what the word 'hate' means," I began to explain. "You see, here in Matthew 5, Jesus says that the word 'hate' means that you wish Mommy and I were dead" (see Matt. 5:21-22).

She took a gulp of a breath and said, "I don't want you or Mommy to die!"

"I know, but Jesus said if you hate somebody, if you hold anger on the inside toward somebody, then you want the person to die."

I've never heard Corynn say the word "hate" since. (Now she has a new phrase: "You and Mommy are mean.")

That may seem like a "tough love" lesson for such a young child, but I want Corynn to know from a young age why it's so important to reconcile relationships and do everything she can to prevent hate from seeping into her relationships with others.

*If you look at the conflict in our world,
you'll realize that it's impossible to live
in peace with everyone. But it is possible to
make every effort to live at peace.*

The apostle Paul says in Romans 12:17-18, "Do not repay anyone evil for evil. Be careful to do what is right in the eyes of everybody. *If it is possible*, as far as it depends on you, live at peace with everyone" (emphasis added).

Notice our emphasis on "as far as it depends on you." It *does* depend on you. Think about the word "you" because *you* are the focus—not the other person. *You* are the one who is to trying to "live at peace with everyone."

You may be wondering, *Is that even possible?*

If you look at the conflict in our world, you'll realize that it's impossible to live in peace with everyone. But it *is* possible to *make every effort* to live at peace. Some people will never forgive you. They will never let go. You may have met with them a dozen times trying to resolve the situation, but there's still no reconciliation. But you tried! You made it your goal to be at peace with them, and that's what God desires.

In my own life, I have had many confrontational situations. I've already told you the basic story about my first pastorate when there was a vote taken as to whether or not I should leave my position there. Although the vote to remove me as pastor did not pass and I left the church six weeks after the vote, it took more than a year for us to work through the surrounding issues. We (the church leadership and me) met with professional counselors. We met with mediators. We went through long battles. And at the end of the day, we kept coming back to this verse from Romans about being at peace with one another. I was challenged by fellow pastors and mentors not to even consider leaving until I had taken every possible approach to reconcile the situation. Only then could I move on. At the time, that lesson was tough, but God has used it to grow me over the past six years as the pastor of Woodland Hills Church.

No matter what painful situation you may be facing today with your spouse, have you done everything you possibly can to resolve it? Have you made every effort to reconcile?

What Breaks the Cycle of Anger

How do you break out of the cycle of anger? It culminates with thanking God for the opportunity to give up what you're feeling and let Him take care of it with His presence. But it begins by recognizing when someone is pushing your buttons and when you're pushing someone else's. So here's the secret: As soon as you feel hurt or tormented, start looking for which of your buttons has been pushed. Then take a moment to pause and pray. What's the underlying issue? Do you feel rejected, controlled or belittled? Do you feel like you have failed, that you'll never succeed or that you can't win?

Now take a deep breath and recognize that you can't change the other person. You can, however, take ownership of the anger in your own heart. Instead of reacting in anger, choose to respond with a blessing. Recognize that the other person probably did not mean to push your button. Instead, God has placed someone in your life to reveal your buttons in order for you to come to terms with them. Without your buttons being pushed, you will not mature or grow or become the person you are meant to become. Take a moment and thank God for the person who is rubbing you the wrong way.

At times I (Gary) pray, "God, thank You for my wife. She has just pushed my button. I appreciate that so much, God. She's a great tool that You are using in my life to help me mature with You."

When you can identify the buttons,
then you diffuse the argument.

I remember one time when I offered an invitation to my daughter that my wife rescinded (for a good reason). But I was suddenly fuming inside. I practiced what we've been talking about in this book—identifying the causes of anger—and I paused, telling myself, *Smalley, she's pushing both of your core fears: being controlled and being belittled.* As Norma continued talking to my daughter, I prayed this prayer: "Lord, I thank You that I can work on only myself. It's *my* control issue. But I want *You* to control me because then I have the best life possible. I want to remain humble (a little branch of the Vine) because that's when You give me more of Your grace. So, thank You for a wife who continually reminds me of my best walk with You." After I prayed I felt so grateful for the reminders my wife brings to me about my need for Christ to remain my King and in control of my life.

After you pause to pray, you're ready to gently let the other person know that your buttons are being pushed. Then find out if you're pushing any buttons. When you can identify the buttons, then you diffuse the argument. Instead of escalating the thoughts that can lead to anger, you are free to look for resolution and reconnection.

In the upcoming chapter, you'll discover eight tools—choices, actually—to help you nurture your emotions and change the way you understand and respond to conflict. These choices will help strengthen your marriage and all of your relationships.

From GarySmalley.com

Q: *I know I have several unresolved anger issues, but I don't know how to get "unstuck." I pray to God, but I get so caught up in anger and feelings of being taken advantage of that I definitely feel stuck in a rut. Any suggestions?*

A: Unresolved anger in your soul is like you drinking poison and hoping another person gets sick. If your actions and reactions are rooted in the behaviors of others, you are only holding yourself hostage from all that God has planned for you.

Respond to God instead of reacting to people. Not a single person on Earth can control you or your feelings, which determine your actions and words. Solomon says to "Guard your heart, for it is the wellspring of life" (Prov. 4:23). Your heart is shaped by what you think about all day long. *You* get to choose what you think about all day long.

You can either live in the negative or live in the positive. You can dwell on negative feelings and thoughts of anger, resentment and get-even tactics. Or you can take the words of the apostle Paul when he says, "Whatever is true, whatever is noble, whatever is right, whatever is pure, whatever is lovely, whatever is admirable—if anything is excellent or praiseworthy—think about such things" (Phil. 4:8).

Have you ever gotten stuck in a conversation and were unable to express your true feelings? Communicating your feelings can be difficult when you feel stuck. "Stuckness" makes you feel incompetent with words. If you go into a conversation expecting things to flow easily and without a lot of effort, you're just kidding yourself. We recommend that you adjust your expectations in three key areas:

First, expect problems and misunderstandings. Even the best communicators sometimes fail to understand others or fall short of making themselves understood. Keep in mind that we're all human. Often we don't even know for sure why we act or feel a certain way.

Second, expect that you'll need a lot of patience. Effective communication takes time. Be careful. Recognize that effective communication deserves patience and a deliberate attempt to understand not only the words being said but also the emotions behind the words. Slow down until you get that.

Third, expect a lot of trial and error. People have different ways of communicating. While all of us can master and use a powerful set of tools for effective communication, the way we use those tools varies from person to person—and that requires trial and error.

You get to make the choice. Others cannot control your thoughts or feelings; you do that. God created you for His purposes, and being stuck is not part of His plan. Work through your feelings. Guard your heart and watch your life change. Your heart is the key.

5

Nurture

Caring for Your Emotions

Whenever you face trials or conflict, sooner or later your emotions will surface. You may feel angry, upset, disappointed, depressed or discouraged. But if you look at your trials or conflicts as opportunities to grow your faith and mature as an individual, you can't help but grow stronger through adversity.

Norma and I (Gary) recently celebrated our forty-third wedding anniversary. Each year, we like to go somewhere special.

A few years ago, she wanted to visit a place she told me had always been a secret desire of hers: a particular historic hotel in the Virgin Islands that was known for its seven gorgeous beaches. I wanted to help fulfill my wife's lifelong dream of visiting this resort, so we saved up and invited two other couples to go with us.

When we arrived at the airport, the couple who was flying with us announced, "We have some good news and some bad news."

I looked at them quizzically.

They went on: "Our other friends [who had flown ahead] decided they didn't like the resort because they don't have any phones and the swimming pool is closed."

I looked at Norma. I knew she was thinking, *When there are seven beaches, who cares about a swimming pool?* and *Who needs a phone on vacation?* This was our anniversary, and Norma had been dreaming about this resort.

Then our traveling companions gave us the "good" news: The couple who had flown ahead had cancelled our prepaid reservation and booked all three couples at the Ritz Carlton on another Island.

Norma's and my stomachs turned into knots. Our friends were millionaires, so they didn't care about the cost, but I was more than a little concerned. Unfortunately, there wasn't time to track down our friends at the Ritz Carlton, so we boarded the plane. We both felt sick the entire flight.

When we landed, we got news that Hurricane Jean was going to hit us the next day. With rain beating down, Norma refused to leave the room. We wanted to try some famous restaurants in the area in honor of our anniversary, but they were all closed.

By the second day, the electricity was off and the hotel was flooded. The toilets stopped working. The water was contaminated. Room service had to bring buckets of water to flush the toilets . . . at the Ritz Carlton. By day four, we received notice that we had to move to another hotel. When the storm finally cleared, it was time to fly home.

We both felt terrible about the situation—about the change in plans, about the hurricane and about paying for a horrible vacation on the "wrong" island. But somewhere in the middle of that week, I woke up to the reality of God in my life.

Remember what I said in the previous chapter about being grateful for the opportunity to let go of what rose up in me when my buttons were pushed so that I could let God fill me with more of Himself? Well, in the middle of that "vacation," I remembered a handful of passages, including 2 Corinthians 12:9-10, which is about taking control of my own thinking.

Here's what I began to acknowledge in my mind: *I know that I am a child of God, and because I am His child, the Holy Spirit lives inside of me. He gives me the power to think the things I should think—rather than the things I am thinking.*

I know that I am a child of God,
and because I am His child,
the Holy Spirit lives inside of me.
He gives me the power to think those
things I should think—rather than
the things I am thinking.

I made a conscious choice to choose my words wisely and stop complaining. I made a conscious choice to praise God in the middle of the trial. I began to thank Him for the work He was doing in me, and began saying out loud: "God, thank You that You are developing more character in me right this moment as I 'suffer' in the hurricane. Thank You for giving me more of Your love, and for enlarging the power of the Holy Spirit inside of me." I actually became grateful for the maturity that was taking place inside of me, just as He promised.

My attitude began to change my actions. I decided to go to the beach—yes, in the middle of the hurricane. I put on my wetsuit and snorkeling gear and found a quiet cove sheltered somewhat by the terrible wind. I enjoyed some of the underwater beauty of God's creation. (Granted, on the way there and back, I had to duck from a few flying objects . . . but it was well worth it.)

For the rest of this chapter, we will describe eight fundamental principles that hold true for all human beings and require choices that determine the outcome of life. Look at these fundamental principles as the beneficial opportunities they are to nurture your emotions and change the way you respond to relationship challenges that come your way.

Eight Opportunities to Nurture Your Emotions

1. As You Think in Your Heart, So You Are

Your thoughts are more important than you realize, because as you think in your heart, so you are. In other words, what you think about yourself affects your decisions, interactions and your emotions.

If you think of yourself as a failure, then when you try something new, more often than not, you may fail. By thinking of yourself as a failure, you set yourself up to be a failure and feel the resulting emotions of discouragement, disappointment and even depression. Likewise, if you think of yourself as someone who gives in to sin or self-destructive behavior, then more often than not, you're going to behave in such a way that supports that belief. If you think of yourself as worthless, incompetent, always late or unintelligent, then you will only see the behavior in yourself that supports these beliefs, and your resulting emotions will include anger and bitterness.

By studying Scripture and memorizing passages, you can literally reprogram your thoughts to think on things that are good and true and honorable and beautiful.

That is why it's so important to think the thoughts that God says He thinks about you. By studying Scripture and memorizing passages, you can literally reprogram your thoughts to think on things that are good and true and honorable and beautiful. Your emotions will follow. You can begin claiming the promises of God in your life. Before you know it, you'll be amazed at how your attitude and relationships will change for the better.

2. What You Think About Affects Your Emotions
While in college, I read a book by a German psychiatrist named Viktor Frankl who was placed in a concentration camp. He wrote something I'll never forget: "The one thing

you can't take away from me is the way I choose to respond to what you do to me. The last of one's freedoms is to choose one's attitude in any given circumstance."

Viktor Frankl tapped into a powerful truth: It's not what happens to you that affects your emotions, it's how you respond. You may have an emotional reaction to an event or interaction, but that emotional reaction is temporary and short-lived. The real emotional legacy is established when you respond to the situation. It may take a little time, but you *can* make good choices that lead to healthy responses. Creating space from the environment or circumstances will allow you to process what is taking place in your heart.

Unfortunately, all too often we find ourselves rehearsing events as we lay in bed. Did you know that in the United States, 1 out of 3 people have experienced insomnia (sleeplessness) at some point in their life? More than 70 million Americans suffer from disorders of sleep and wakefulness. While many of these cases are related to physical disorders or too much caffeine, our experience indicates that many are directly related to anger left unchecked.[1]

Stress can easily lead to anger. Solomon speaks about sleeplessness caused by stress over money:

Whoever loves money never has money enough; whoever loves wealth is never satisfied with his income. This too is meaningless. As goods increase, so do those who consume them. And what benefit are they to the owner except to feast his eyes on them?

The sleep of a laborer is sweet, whether he eats little or much, but the abundance of a rich man permits him no sleep (Eccles. 5:10-12).

The image here is of a wealthy man lying down at night counting his flocks and planning the next day's business. Not that owning stuff is bad; but the more you have, the more you have to think about. The more you think, the more your emotions are likely to run amiss.

The more I (Ted) study Scripture, the more convinced I become that God wants me to get a good night's sleep. Worse than caffeine, unresolved anger and conflict have caused many sleepless nights for me.

My mind has a very difficult time shutting off at night. As a pastor, a writer with deadlines, a marriage and family speaker, a daddy, a husband, a son and a friend, most nights when my head hits the pillow, I simply say, "Lord, You are going to have to take care of things for the next 8 hours or so. I need some rest." (I say that tongue-in-cheek, knowing that God takes care of things 24/7. But that prayer has worked better than Nyquil on more than one night.)

Some people allow their anger to turn to evil plotting and scheming about how they can get even the very next day. The prophet Micah pointed out the sleeplessness of the leaders of Judah and called them to integrity:

Woe to those who plan iniquity, to those who plot evil on their beds! At morning's light they carry it out because it is in their power to do it (Mic. 2:1).

Have you ever laid your head on the pillow with thoughts of revenge toward another person? Your immediate answer may be no, but think about it: Have you ever rehearsed a conversation in your head at night and thought of a few more "zingers" or arguments you could use to get even?

Unresolved anger is quick to plot evil late at night. Maybe it is for this reason that God challenges us: "Do not let the sun go down while you are still angry" (Eph. 4:26). It is as much for your wellbeing as it is for the wellbeing of your relationship.

A sound, peaceful, loving and forgiving spirit will give you great rest. If your anger permits you no sleep, don't spend thousands of dollars on a new mattress; instead, turn your anger over to the Lord. Follow the prescription from Proverbs 3:21-24:

> My son, preserve sound judgment and discernment, do not let them out of your sight; they will be life for you, an ornament to grace your neck. Then you will go on your way in safety, and your foot will not stumble; when you lie down, you will not be afraid; when you lie down, your sleep will be sweet.

Will you allow yourself to rehearse the same emotional turmoil, or will you turn things around by recognizing that no situation is beyond God's redemption? No matter what you've been through, God can use you to bring healing to others—but only after you've experienced healing yourself.[2]

Can you think of three people in your life
that irritate you on a regular basis? They are
some of the best tools God has right now to
help shape you into who you're created to be.

The "Miracle-Gro" of personal development is pain and trials. And usually the "pain and trials" have faces. Can you think of three people in your life that irritate you on a regular basis? They are some of the best tools God has right now to help shape you into who you're created to be. If you want the character of Christ in you, then every trial and every difficult person is an opportunity for growth toward maturity.

3. You Are 100-Percent Empowered to Control Your Own Thoughts

Whether you realize it or not, you are 100-percent responsible for all of your thoughts. Nobody else controls your thoughts—only you. No matter what experience you've been through, no matter how horrible the details—at the end of the day, you have a choice to make: Are you going to be bitter or are you going to be better?

The truth is that you are not a victim. No matter what has happened to you, it's what you think about what happened to you that will shape you and your future. And you alone are the one who controls those thoughts and the resulting emotions.

When people begin taking responsibility for their thoughts, it can transform a family, a community and even a society. Just imagine a 12-year-old girl who says to her mom, "I have now accepted the ownership of being solely responsible for all of my own thoughts. If dinner isn't good, you won't hear me complaining, because you're not responsible for my thoughts or my feelings or my words or my actions. I am responsible."

Now think of an example from your own life that would improve the atmosphere in your home if you started telling yourself to take ownership of your feelings whenever your spouse did something or said something that deviated from your expectations. (Trust us, it will get easier as you practice doing it.)

We are all responsible for the way we choose to feel. Bad, unpleasant or less-than-ideal things may happen to us. We do not deny them. But we do not allow them to define us. We take 100-percent responsibility for our thoughts and the emotions that result from those thoughts.

4. You Have Unlimited Access to Love, Peace and Hope

When you accept Jesus Christ as your Lord and Savior, the Scriptures say that the Holy Spirit takes up residence inside of you. He gives you unlimited access to love, peace and hope. You have unlimited access to the power to overcome whatever you're facing in this world. No trial is too hard. No challenge is too big. No situation is too difficult. You can overcome because all things are possible through Christ who strengthens you (see Phil. 4:13).

That means your emotions do not have to run wild or get the best of you. You can take control of them through the power of God's Spirit living inside of you.

5. You Have Power to Take Every Thought, Belief, Dream and Idea Captive

For years, I (Gary) empowered everyone around me to control my emotions—including family, friends, coworkers, food servers and even the people on the other end of the telephone line who put me on hold. This was never more true than when I traveled.

At one particular hotel, I had reserved a room on the first floor. When I looked at the room key, I realized that I had been put on the third floor.

"Let me show you the reservation," I said, interrupting the desk clerk's conversation with the next person in line.

"Sir, I'm helping this other customer," she responded. "Could you wait just a moment?"

Inside, anger was beginning to build. *I made the reservation for the first floor and now we're on the third. This woman is wrong*, I thought to myself.

At that moment, the guy behind me in line tapped me on the shoulder and asked, "Hey, aren't you Gary Smalley?"

I nodded and smiled, but inside I felt the weight of conviction. I had let my thoughts and emotions run wild. I shouldn't have interrupted the woman. I shouldn't have gotten so upset. I had given the people around me power to control my emotions.

As a child of God, I have the power to take every thought, belief, dream and idea captive to the obedience of Christ. (So do you!) But at that point, I didn't realize I had that power and could manage myself by what I believed about every situation.

One of the biggest keys to taking control of our thought and emotional life is to follow the instruction of Colossians 3:17: "Set your minds on things above, not on earthly things." One translation suggests that when we give up our expectations of the things on this earth, we have our expectations met from above. When we combine this idea with the heart of John 15 (He is the Vine, we are the branches on the Vine), we understand that when we're connected to the source of life, He gives us all we need. He can use the difficulties we face every day to build us to contain more of His love.

One of the best exercises for setting your affections on things above is to take out a few sheets of blank paper and begin writing down every expectation in your life—in your marriage, your family, your relationships, your work, your future. I recently did this and filled up four-and-a-half pages! I wrote what I expect Norma to do and be. I wrote down expectations for each of my children and for their spouses. I wrote down expectations for our ministry and our future. I wrote down expectations regarding my health and my fitness levels. I even wrote down my expectations for airlines, hotel and rental car companies. I wrote down everything I could think of . . . and then I wadded up the pages and laid them at the foot of the Cross.

"Lord Jesus, I give You all my expectations of this earth," I prayed. "Because You have given me power and love and fulfillment and life, I don't need any of these expectations anyway. Lord, I take all expectations and hand them over to You."

Do you know what happened? My stress level dropped immediately. Emotional hurts and disappointments disappeared. Past wounds began to be healed. I found myself living with a new sense of peace and gratitude. Joy overflowed from my heart.

I still have dreams and hopes and goals, but they are more surrendered to God than they have ever been. As a result, my faith is stronger, and I believe that God can do far greater things than anything I could do on my own.

When you take your thoughts, beliefs, dreams and ideas captive to Christ, you get more than you ever give up. (You don't have to write down all your expectations and then wad up the paper like I did, but sometimes doing something physical like that promotes positive change more quickly.)

6. Make the Words You Speak Honorable and Wholesome

Did you hear about the freshman girl who was about to finish her first year of college? In a few weeks, she would be home. She decided to write her parents a letter. She wrote:

Dear Mother and Dad,

Since I left for college I have been remiss in writing and I am sorry for my thoughtlessness in not having written before. I will bring you up to date now, but before you read on, please sit down. You are not to read any further unless you are sitting down, okay?

Well, then, I am getting along pretty well now. The skull fracture and the concussion I got when I jumped out the window of my dormitory when it caught on fire shortly after my arrival here is pretty well healed now. I only spent two weeks in the hospital and now I can see almost normally and only get those sick headaches once a day. Fortunately, the fire in the dormitory, and my jump, were witnessed by an attendant at the gas station near the dorm; he was the one who called the fire department and the ambulance. He also visited me in the hospital, and since I had nowhere to live because of the burnt out dormitory, he was kind enough to invite me to share his apartment with him. It's really a basement room, but it's kind of cute. He is a very fine boy and we have fallen deeply in love and are planning to get married. We haven't got the exact date yet, but it will be before my pregnancy begins to show.

Yes, Mother and Dad, I am pregnant. I know how much you are looking forward to being grandparents, and I know you will welcome the baby and give it the same love and devotion and tender care you gave me when I was a child. The reason for the delay in our marriage is that my boyfriend has a minor infection that prevents us from passing our premarital blood tests, and I carelessly caught it from him.

Now that I have brought you up to date, I want to tell you that there was no dormitory fire; I did not have a con-

cussion or skull fracture; I was not in the hospital; I am not pregnant; I am not engaged; I am not infected; and there is no boyfriend. However, I am getting a "D" in American History and an "F" in Chemistry, and I want you to see those marks in their proper perspective.

Your loving daughter,

Sharon[3]

Imagine the wide range of emotions her parents felt as they read this letter from their daughter. Isn't it amazing the power words have on our emotions? The words we choose, the way we choose to express them and even the order of the ideas we present have emotional implications.

The words you speak are more important than you realize! That's why James 3:2 says, "If you can control your tongue, you are mature and able to control your whole body" (*CEV*). If that is your goal, it is important to make the words you speak honorable and wholesome. But you can't control your words by yourself alone, and that's why God gave us James 4:6: "God opposes the proud [those who think they can live the best life without God], but gives grace to the humble."

I use Galatians 5:22-23 as a grid for the words I speak. This passage highlights the fruit of the Spirit: love, joy, peace, long-suffering, gentleness, goodness, faith, meekness and temperance. I try to run through each characteristic before I speak and ask myself, *Does what I want to say show love? Joy? Peace? Long-suffering? Gentleness? Goodness? Faith? Meekness? Temperance?* If the answer is no to any of the above, then I know that whatever is on my mind is better left unsaid. I cannot tell you how many relationship blunders I have avoided by remembering this one passage in Scripture.

When the words you speak are honorable and wholesome, you nurture your emotions and breathe life into your own soul.

7. Celebrate Both the Trials and the Joy that Will Soon Be Yours

Romans 5:3 says that you can exult—I mean pom-pom time—when something difficult happens; and James 1 says that when you start going through a trial, you should start thinking about how much joy you're in for in just a matter of hours or days. That is God's promise. Why would we be discouraged when we go through a trial? We are going to get a lot of joy!

A few years ago, someone stole my computer carry-on case, which was in the church where I was speaking. The computer had all of my speaking notes, the book I was working on and several years' worth of research. Even worse, the bag had a special anniversary necklace and ring I had purchased for Norma. When I realized the bag was gone, I was flooded with negative thoughts and fears. I wondered what personal files were on my laptop's hard drive. I wondered how I was going to meet the deadline for my next book. I wondered what Norma would say when I told her that her anniversary gift had been stolen.

Then I stopped my mind in its tracks. I began clinging to the promise of God that with every trial, joy will come.

I began thanking God. I prayed out loud, "God, thank You for this trial. It's massive, and I feel terrible about it, but thank You for allowing me with Your power to control my thoughts."

Do you know what happened? My attitude changed. My stress level decreased. I felt the weight of the moment lift. My stomach even calmed down. Not only did I take control of my thoughts, but I also took control of my emotions. That's because emotions are "data" that tell us what we have been thinking over the past few hours or days.

8. Learn to Boast in Your Weaknesses

Why is boasting in your weaknesses so important to nurturing your emotions? Because hiding your weaknesses takes a whole lot of emotional and mental energy that leaves you drained and exhausted. Instead of hiding your weaknesses, boast in the fact that God is in the business of redeeming you, strengthening you and using your weakness for His glory.

Instead of hiding your weaknesses,
boast in the fact that God is in the business
of redeeming you, strengthening you and
using your weakness for His glory.

I believe that's what the apostle Paul had in mind when he wrote, "But he said to me, 'My grace is sufficient for you, for my power is made perfect in weakness.' Therefore I will boast all the more gladly about my weaknesses, so that Christ's power may rest on me. That is why, for Christ's sake, I delight in weaknesses, in insults, in hardships, in persecutions, in difficulties. For when I am weak, then I am strong" (2 Cor. 12:9-10).

Paul learned to find delight in his weaknesses, and I am learning to do the same. One of my weaknesses is that I am dyslexic. I reverse things continually. I have tried different doctors' recommendations for the condition, but nothing has ever helped. Though I was embarrassed by this weakness as a kid, I boast in it today.

Another weakness is that I'm not academically inclined. Even from an early age, school was never easy for me. I failed the third grade. In fact, I never took a book home until my senior year in high school. I had convinced myself that I was stupid, so there was no reason to even try. Even to this day, I can only type about 25 words a minute, and by the time I finish a single line there are almost a dozen mistakes.

Yet I boast in these weaknesses. Why? Because to date, I have written more than 55 books, which together have sold more than 10 million copies. I know that success is not my own; I know that it's all because of God and His goodness. I can now see how God has used my weakness for His glory. For instance, I still score at a sixth-grade level of reading and spelling. Do you know why it's easy for me to "boast" in those weaknesses? Because self-improvement and relationship books sell best when they are written on a sixth-grade level. God has used me to help a ton of people over the years through sixth-grade level books!

Because of my academic challenges, one of my gifts is taking complicated things and making them simple. Why? Because I'm simple. People from all over the world connect with my message, because I talk about my weaknesses, struggles and mistakes in an easy-to-understand way. I used to be so embarrassed by my weaknesses, but now I've learned to boast in them.

If you're going to boast in anything, boast in your weaknesses. Not only is it good for your humility, it's also good for your emotional health.

The antidote for anger is, ultimately, forgiveness. In the next chapter, we explore the three essentials of forgiveness and the five keys to cultivating a forgiving spirit.

From GarySmalley.com

Q: My dad and mom are no longer living and I still have a hard time forgiving them for divorcing when I was 11. I have held it in for my entire life and feel as though much of the grief in my life is a direct result of the poor example set by my folks. How can I forgive dead parents and move on with my life?

A: Your question is a great start to recovery. You need to move on and no longer blame your mom and dad for shortcomings in your life.

Paul advised, "Do not repay anyone evil for evil. Be careful to do what is right in the eyes of everybody. If it is possible, as far as it depends on you, live at peace with everyone"

(Rom. 12:17-18). The verse says, *"as far as it depends on you."* It is no longer possible for you to be face to face with your mom and dad, but you can still forgive them. Not for their sake, but for yours. You need to rid your body of the poison you have been drinking called bitterness and resentment.

The issue of forgiveness is at the core of personal responsibility. Your anger and unforgiveness toward your mom and dad have held you back. Your victim's approach to life has thwarted God's best for you.

Release the hurt. Release the past. Once you turn this over to the Lord, you will then be able to live at peace with everyone. You will no longer be held hostage or be powerless in life. You will change once you begin to resolve your anger.

Here are three critical steps toward resolving your anger:

1. *Receive.* To stay healthy, you have to receive from others. There are resources God wants to give you through the help and assistance of others. You must open your heart to Him and to others in order to receive what you need. To practice good self-care, you must learn to let the love of God and others penetrate. You must allow God's love to sink into your soul. You must receive.

2. *Attend.* Caring for yourself is biblical and honors Gods. Learn to listen to what your emotions are telling you about your circumstances. Remember, your feelings provide information essential for effective self-care.

3. *Give.* When you keep in mind that God made you for relationships, you bring balance to your life and avoid selfishness. Why? Because you realize that you must take care of yourself to have something to give to others.

Let me say it as strongly as possible: There's no way you can take care of yourself without truly giving and serving others. If you're not giving—if you're focused only on receiving—then you're working against your own best interests.

Receiving, attending, giving—if any one of these is missing, you'll develop a big hole in one of your main relationships: with God, with others or with yourself. But when you pay careful attention to all three, you set yourself up to develop deep, lasting, fulfilling relationships in all walks of life.

Notes

1. SleepMed Insomnia Statistics, http://www.sleepmed.md/page/1896 (accessed June 2008).

2. You can read the complete explanation of this concept in Gary's book, *Change Your Heart, Change Your Life* (Nashville, TN: Thomas Nelson Publishers, 2008).

3. Robert B. Cialdini, *Influence: The Psychology of Persuasion* (New York: Collins, 1st Collins Business Essentials Ed edition, 2006).

6

Liberate

Embracing the Spirit of Forgiveness

The power to forgive is one of the most amazing powers God gives us. Nowhere is this truer than in marriage! Not only can forgiveness transform your marriage, but it can also transform your life and the hearts of those around you.

In the previous chapter, we gave you eight tools (or choices) to help you nurture your emotions and change the way you understand and respond to trials in your life. Now we want to go one step further and help you walk in the fullness of what it means to forgive. In this chapter, we look at three nonnegotiable essentials of forgiveness, as well as five keys to cultivating a forgiving spirit.

Forgiveness: How Many Times?

In the book of Matthew, we read that Peter approached Jesus to ask Him a very serious question: He wanted to know if there is any limit to forgiveness. Peter drew on what he had learned from the rabbis of the day. Namely, that if a man committed an offense once, you were always to forgive him. If a man committed a second and third offense, you were to forgive him again. But on the fourth offense, you were not to forgive. This belief was based on a passage in Amos where God pronounced on the enemies of Israel that for three sins, even four, He would pour out his wrath on the enemy nation (see Amos 1–2).

Drawing on this teaching, Peter approached Jesus and doubled the amount of forgiveness he had been taught: "Lord, how many times shall I forgive my brother when he sins against me? Up to seven times?" Peter thought he was being generous, but Jesus responded, "I tell you, not seven times, but seventy-seven times" (Matt. 18:21-22). Jesus used hyperbolic language; 490 times (77 times, meaning 70 times 7) represents limitless forgiveness. Your forgiveness toward someone who offends you must have no limits.

Forgiveness is me giving up the right
to hurt you for hurting me.

One of the best definitions of forgiveness we've ever heard is this: *Forgiveness is me giving up the right to hurt you for hurting me.* Rather than wanting to get even, I want to help you. Even though I have a right to hurt you back because you offended me, I give up that right. I respond rather than react.

When you give up the right to hurt someone because he (she) has hurt you, you know that God is working within you—after all, none of us feels like giving up our rights, right? Each time you forgive your spouse, God grows in you a little more of His character. You forgive as He forgives!

Three Essential Elements of Forgiveness

Forgiveness is the greatest attribute that you can cultivate in your character because it's one of the greatest attributes of God. When you forgive, you emulate the very character of God. No one demonstrated true forgiveness more beautifully than Jesus Christ. On the cross, after being beaten, spit upon, unjustly accused, nailed to a cross and killed, He said, "Forgive them, for they do not know what they are doing" (Luke 23:34). Throughout the Bible we read of men and women who chose to forgive. Stephen, an early Christian, asked God to forgive his murderers of their sin even as he was being stoned to death. That kind of action doesn't come from natural man—it's supernatural and comes from God.

If you really want to forgive your spouse, or anyone else in your life, there are three essentials—no limits, no remembrance, no hanging on—to keep in mind. These are not optional; they are nonnegotiable. Real forgiveness requires the following:

1. No Limits

This is crucial. You cannot place any limits on your forgiveness. Real forgiveness does not have requirements or contingencies, and it does not have to be earned. It is freely given. There cannot be any limits to your forgiveness—especially when it comes to your spouse. No matter what has happened, you are invited to forgive just as God has wholly and fully forgiven you. Where do you find that kind of forgiveness? Through the person of Jesus Christ. Matthew 10:8 says, "Freely you have received, freely give." Notice that you cannot give unless you have received. You are to forgive because Christ forgave you. You are to give freely out of the well of forgiveness from which you have received.

You are to give freely out of the well of forgiveness from which you have received.

If you are not a forgiving person—if you have unresolved anger, bitterness or resentment in your heart—and you do nothing to get rid of it, then you have not yet experienced or realized the forgiveness you have received in Christ Jesus. And because God has given us the design to live by, you will face the natural consequences of violating His will by not forgiving others.

Many times we want to put conditions on our forgiveness. We say things like, "I'll forgive you if you promise never to do this again" or "When he shows some remorse, then I'll know he is ready to be forgiven" or "It won't do any good; she won't change." These statements fail to understand that forgiveness is far more than just a tool to restore relationships. It is also a tool to restore our own souls.

As we wrote earlier, there may be times when it is not possible to reconcile a relationship with a family member who is no longer living. Funerals are generally where that reality hits the hardest, which is why I often teach on forgiveness at these services.

The more you limit yourself in giving out forgiveness, the more limits you place on your life. Did you know that the quality of your life hinges on your ability to forgive with no limits? Understanding that fact alone will change your walk with Christ forever.

2. No Remembrance

When it comes to forgiveness, you also must choose to forget the sin against you, and refuse to rehearse or replay the situation through your mind. Don't keep mentioning the incident to your spouse. You have to let it go. Forgetting is a choice, and it's a choice that God makes with you every day. If you find it difficult to forget the offenses against you, try what I (Gary) do: Rehearse how many times you've sinned against God and been forgiven, then realize that what was done to you does not even come close to what you have done to God and to others in the past. It's so much easier to forgive and forget when we remember our own sins. If the memory of an offense keeps coming back, use it to remind yourself of your sins and of how gracious God is in forgiving you.

Psalm 103:12 says, "As far as the east is from the west, so far has he removed our transgressions from us." Think about that! If you go north, eventually you'll cross over the North Pole and head south. But if you go east, you will never head west. God is saying that you are forgiven. Period.

My wife, Amy, is a teacher for me (Ted) of this kind of forgiving forgetfulness. When we get into disagreements, Amy does not get hysterical, but neither does she get historical. By "historical" I'm referring to when a person recalls every detail of every past failure with great precision and submits them as evidence into every discussion or fight. Like a lawyer submitting a list of prior offenses to the jury, it's tempting to bolster our case in the present disagreement with the past. But remember, "Love keeps no record of wrongs" (1 Cor. 13:5).

The most common trait of the historical mate is exaggeration. An exaggerator is quickly spotted by his or her frequent use of the words "always" and "never." The exaggerator's statements look like this:

"You always come home late."

"You never take out the trash."

"You always just sit on your duff and watch TV."

"You never want to talk about it."

Those statements make some pretty big assumptions. Even if you are home on time 9 times out of 10, the exaggerating spouse can make it seem as if you are late five days a week. You may take the trash out 99 times out of 100, but forget once and your historical mate goes through the roof and remembers the 6 times between the years of 1990 and 1993 when you forgot to take out the trash. That is a mate who is not living with a forgiving spirit.

"Only the brave know how to forgive. A coward never forgives. It's not in his nature."
ROBERT MULLER

3. No Hanging On

A story is told that when Leonardo da Vinci was painting *The Last Supper*, he got into a fight with a fellow painter. He got so angry that he painted the face of that painter on Judas's body. But when he went to paint the face of Christ, he couldn't do it—he was harboring bitterness and anger in his heart. Da Vinci erased the painter's face from Judas's body so that he could finish his masterpiece.

When it comes to forgiveness, you cannot forgive 99 percent and leave 1 percent unforgiven; you have to forgive completely. That's what Jesus did on the cross. Through His sacrifice, He didn't offer forgiveness only for some sins or most sins; He provided forgiveness for *all* sins.

Several years ago, Gary and I were fishing for brown trout on Lake Taneycomo, near Branson, Missouri. It was a beautiful day and the fish were biting. We had a small group of five guys, and the poles were busy. A few hours in, Gary hooked the mother of all fish and I committed one of the most egregious acts a fisherman can commit. I was so excited for him that I lost my head in the excitement. As he worked the fish closer, I leaped forward to offer my net. He worked the fish toward me. That's when it happened, something I'll never forgive myself for: I grabbed the line.

If you're a non-fly-fisherman type, let me explain. The reason fly-fishing rods are nine feet long is that they counterbalance the very thin line that is invisible to trout. With a six-foot rod, the fish would break the line every time, but a nine-foot pole takes the pressure off of the line. When I grabbed the line, I rendered Gary's pole useless. The fish (or should I say, the world-record fish) broke off the line. My heart sank. The mother of all brown trout got away. We have never caught that fish ever again. We've quit trying.

Forgiveness that lets go completely works the same way. When the offense breaks off the line, you give up trying to catch it again. You consider it gone. You let the person and the offense off the hook. You refuse to hang on.

What was Gary's response to losing his mountable fish? "No big deal, Ted. Don't give it another thought." (I still think he may have a slight case of unresolved anger over it. There is a blank space on his office wall the exact size of that fish.)

The Forgiveness Tank

I love Beth Moore's book *Get Out of That Pit.*[1] Moore says that we all are tempted to live in the pit. Your pit may be unresolved anger or bitterness and resentment. Your pit may be constant complaining and negativity.

When you make a choice to get out of the pit, you're likely to find that it's tougher than you planned, because the people still in the pit get mad. They don't want you to get out, because they've enjoyed your company. But you know it's time to move on. So you insist on getting out, and you invite them along too. As you're crawling out of the pit, you don't look down on the people still inside. You don't push them down or try to step on their foreheads. Instead, you help those who are willing to get out of the pit.

In order to get out of the pit and help others out as well, you've got to know about and understand your forgiveness tank.

Imagine a large white tank of water, your forgiveness tank. Everyone has one. Your forgiveness tank is where you draw from when someone cuts you off driving down the road. Your forgiveness tank is where you draw from when someone in customer service is rude to you. Your forgiveness tank is a must-have when someone borrows something important to you and breaks it.

You draw from your forgiveness tank not only for people and situations in your life today, but also for those in your past. Make a list of people toward whom you are harboring some form of anger, bitterness, disappointment or frustration. Can you think of any people that you're trying to avoid right now? If so, that's a good sign that you need to draw from your forgiveness tank. All kinds of people may come to mind: your spouse, family members, coworkers, neighbors, kids, past bosses, pastors, small-group leaders or members, childhood friends or bullies.

With each person or encounter you choose to forgive, you empty a little bit of water from your forgiveness tank. You let go of the grudge. You release the anger. You make a commitment to keep no record of wrong.

As you pour out of your forgiveness tank, the water level drops lower and lower. If the tank is not refilled, soon you're running on empty. You keep your forgiveness tank full with the knowledge of how much Christ has forgiven you (and that's a never-ending supply of forgiveness). It's easy to make a critical mistake about forgiveness if you start expecting the people you have forgiven to pour back into you and refill the tank. Without realizing it, you begin to offer conditional forgiveness. You forgive with the silent hope that they will reciprocate, and before you know it, your forgiveness tank runs dry. A hairline crack appears. And once there is nothing left in your forgiveness tank, as well as the damage done to the tank itself, you are slower to forgive and let go.

I know this scenario well, because I've lived it. For years in our marriage, I'd do something foolish and then say, "Amy, I'm sorry, will you forgive me?" In her grace and love, she would say, "I forgive you." I felt better hearing her words, but I also felt like something was missing. In my emptiness I'd then ask, "Is there anything else you would like to say?"

I thought I was asking for forgiveness, but . . . I was not taking the issue to Christ and looking to Him to refill my forgiveness tank with the enjoyment that comes from being forgiven by Him.

Amy would look at me be blankly. I thought I was asking her forgiveness, but really I was asking for her to pour back into me. I was not taking the issue to Christ and looking to Him to refill my forgiveness tank with the enjoyment that comes from being forgiven by Him.

The truth is that you can't generate one drop of love or forgiveness on your own. You can only give what you've received from God. If you sit around waiting for others to fill up your tank, you will be disappointed and disillusioned. Instead of forgiveness, you will harbor anger and frustration. How many times have you expected a relationship or a situation to give life to you? Only Christ, the living Vine, gives us everything we need out of His riches in glory: "In him we have redemption through his blood, the forgiveness of sins, in accordance with the riches of God's grace that he lavished on us with all wisdom and understanding" (Eph. 1:7-8).

I know that it's not easy to keep pouring forgiveness on someone when they don't offer you a drop in return. That's why it's so important to fill up your tank with Christ and the forgiveness He offers you. There will always be people in your life that can't or won't reciprocate, but you don't have to allow them to determine who you are or how you respond. You may be asking for something they simply do not have to give, because they never received it themselves.

I (Ted) experienced this with my Grandma Cunningham, one of the nicest people in the entire state of Pennsylvania. She was one of the most loved people—everyone in the community where she lived had something amazing to say about her. Yet every time we spoke on the phone, I'd say, "Grandma, I love you" toward the end of the conversation and she'd respond with, "Uh-huh."

On more than one occasion, I would hang up the phone feeling troubled. I would turn to my wife and confess, "Just once, I would like to hear the words 'I love you' from my grandmother."

Yet Grandma Cunningham never said it. She passed away a few years ago, and there's still something inside of me that aches to hear her say those words, *I love you.*

No matter what words you've longed to hear—*I forgive you, I love you, I'm proud of you*—there are some people who won't or can't say them. But your forgiveness tank is not based on the other person; it's based on your relationship with God. People are not the ones who can fill you up. That's God's job! Allow Him to be the source of your strength and hope and love and forgiveness. Fill up your forgiveness tank through prayer, worship and studying the Scriptures. Allow God to whisper in your heart, *I forgive you, I love you, I'm proud of you.* When you are replenished and overflowing, you will become a source of life and strength to others. In the process, you'll help them climb out of their pit as well. (Whatever—or whoever—you're thinking about right now in regard to forgiveness, it might be a good time to pray about it.)

Forgiveness Inventory

Are you slow or quick to forgive—with *no limits, no remembrance* and *no hanging on*? To find out, respond to the statements below on a scale of 0 (not true) to 10 (very true) as each applies to you.

____ 1. I have frequent recurring minor health problems.

____ 2. I tend to experience difficulty remaining close to people.

____ 3. I continually fail to see pitfalls in business deals.

____ 4. I have little interest in religious matters.

____ 5. I have many doubts about the existence of God.

____ 6. I tend to see religious people as a bunch of hypocrites.

____ 7. I tend to be judgmental or overly critical of people.

____ 8. Others have described me as "cold."

____ 9. I have a general inability to see my own short-comings.

____ 10. My image—including what I wear and drive—is very important to me.

____ 11. I often struggle with feelings of low self-value.

____ 12. I often fail to see when my words or actions hurt the feelings of others.

____ 13. My parents divorced before I turned 18 years old.

____ 14. I think one or both of my parents drank too much alcohol.

____ 15. My parents seemed to be addicted to drugs or other substances.

___ 16. My parents abused me physically, verbally or sexually.

___ 17. My parents seemed distant or neglectful to me.

___ 18. I felt that my parents were too controlling of me.

___ 19. I often struggle with feelings of discouragement or depression.

___ 20. I seem to be at odds with several people for long periods of time.

___ 21. I tend to be overly controlling of my mate, children or friends.

___ 22. I have general feelings of anxiety, though I can't put my finger on what it is I'm uneasy about.

___ 23. I have sometimes thought about suicide.

___ 24. I have a hard time forgiving others when they hurt or frustrate me.

___ 25. I have a hard time confronting others when they hurt me, and I know I'm not that good at getting my anger out.

___ 26. I find myself overly busy most of the time.

___ 27. I find it easier to blame others than to take responsibility for my mistakes.

___ 28. I often overreact to what others say or do to me.

___ 29. I feel that I'm motivated far too often by fear of failure.

___ 30. I often wish people who have hurt me could be punished.

___ 31. I frequently think that I've been cheated in important areas of life.

___ 32. I get into fights with others that sometimes result in physical aggression, such as throwing things, slapping or hitting.

___ 33. I don't really trust anyone other than myself.

Add up your total score. If your total score is more than 100, spend some time memorizing and meditating on the passages included in the Meditations for Forgiveness at the end of the book. If your score is more than 200, you may want to see a counselor who is trained to help people uncover and deal with anger and find ways to forgive.

Five Keys to Cultivating a Forgiving Spirit

We are called in Scripture to encourage one another and lift each other up. The power of words can do that. There is nothing greater than being in a relationship where both people are operating from a forgiving spirit. Here are five ways to encourage a forgiving spirit in your marriage and stay connected.

1. Be Tender with Your Spouse

Make a decision to seek reconciliation and show your spouse your tender side. How do you do that? Pay attention to your approach. If you come at your spouse and say, "Listen, I need you to take care of this right now," how do you think your spouse will respond? Your words, tone and body language place you on the offensive, which leaves your spouse to play defense. If you find yourself taking the wrong approach, then walk back out of the room and start again. An approach such as, "Honey, if you have a free moment I could really use your help on this" is far more tender and much more effective.

Scientists estimate that the majority of your communication is nonverbal, which means that a significant proportion of the way you communicate is through your face.

When you're communicating with your spouse, remember to use a calm voice—regardless of his or her response. Pay close attention to your facial expressions. Scientists estimate that the majority of a person's communication is nonverbal, which means that a significant proportion of the way you communicate is through your face. Avoid frowning or furrowing your eyebrows. Instead, smile warmly and look your spouse in the eye. Pay attention to your body language: Are your arms crossed or relaxed gently by your side? Look for ways to be soft and tender in your response.

2. Practice Empathy

Nurturing a forgiving spirit in a relationship means desiring to understand the other person above being understood. If you have offended your spouse, try to find out what's at the core of the offense. Here's a little secret: You can find out the core issue by asking the right questions. Resist the temptation to defend yourself and instead focus on how you can restore and reconcile the relationship. Remove words like "but" and "I" as you treasure hunt for the truth of what's happened.

When you care enough to find out what happened and why, your empathy establishes a foundation for reconciliation.

When you're treasure hunting, you may hear some unpleasant things. You may hear phrases such as, "I felt like you didn't really care for me," or "I felt like I wasn't really important to you," or "I felt like your work was more important than our family" or "I felt that you were being selfish and manipulative." Those kinds of words can be hard to hear, but continue to approach the situation with gentleness. When you care enough to find out what happened and why it happened, your empathy establishes a foundation for reconciliation.

3. Affirm Hurt and Admit Any Wrong

No matter what the situation, everyone has a different perspective. For instance, the things that make my five-year-old daughter cry don't make me cry. I can walk in and out of Target without buying a toy and be just fine. My daughter cannot. The pain or loss she experiences is very real to her. It's all a matter of perspective.

In nurturing a spirit of forgiveness, words and attitudes determine the speed of reconciliation. That's why you need to eliminate certain phrases from your vocabulary, such as, "If I offended you, I'm sorry" and "You shouldn't have felt that way." Those kinds of statements deny the pain or distress the other person has experienced and block the road to forgiveness.

Instead of denying or dismissing a person's woundedness, a forgiving spirit acknowledges the pain and admits any wrong in provoking his or her hurt. So instead of offering quips such as, "That's crazy," "I was just kidding" or "Get over it," admit to the pain you have caused the person and ask for his or her forgiveness.

4. Touch Gently

Nurturing a spirit of forgiveness means using gentle touch when appropriate. A UCLA study once revealed that for a person to be successful and physically healthy in life, they need 8 to 10 touches each day. That doesn't mean you go to your wife and touch her on the arm with your finger while you count to 10. That's not a gentle touch. Place your hand on your spouse's shoulder, knee or hand and squeeze lightly—that is both gentle and disarming.

A gentle touch can go a long way toward preventing conflict and building a healthy relationship. The importance of gentle touch has been noted even in infants. An experiment was once conducted with 50 infants to determine what language they would speak if never permitted to hear the spoken word. A foster mother was assigned to each child, but the women were forbidden to touch or talk to the babies. The experiment failed because every infant died.

Today, scientists have confirmed just how important touch is to babies' survival and wellbeing. Gentle touch is critical to the survival of your relationships as well. Establishing a connection of touch can close the distance between you and your spouse, defusing anger and inviting a spirit of forgiveness.

5. Seek Forgiveness and Wait for a Response

Even though you follow the first four keys to nurturing a spirit of forgiveness, you may not receive forgiveness right away. If you have been soft and tender, listened to your spouse, admitted any wrongdoing and touched him or her gently as a sign of care, you may believe that you deserve a response right on the spot. But some people won't be ready or able to provide one. They need time to process everything, and that's okay.

You may do everything right when it comes to seeking forgiveness yet not be forgiven by the other person. Or, you may do everything right and receive forgiveness but nothing more. You may wonder what went wrong.

Rest assured that if you've done everything you can to seek forgiveness, then you're doing things right. You cannot control what someone else thinks or feels, but you can control your own emotions. When you choose to reconcile, you are choosing freedom for yourself.

Who do you need to forgive? Is there anyone who is holding a grudge against you? Maybe there is a friendship from your past that turned sour. Maybe there is a family member you haven't spoken to in months or even years. Maybe there is something between you and your spouse that needs to be resolved.

We want to encourage you today to take the first step. Spend some time in prayer and study and fill up your forgiveness tank. Prayerfully begin using the five keys to nurturing a spirit of forgiveness and see how you—and your relationships—begin to change with God's help.

In the next chapter, we equip you with one of the most powerful tools for embracing forgiveness: a well-crafted, heartfelt apology. Asking someone to forgive you is more than just saying, "I'm sorry."

From GarySmalley.com

Q: *My wife and I almost separated and divorced about two weeks ago. Thank God we decided to try to make a go of our relationship. We love each other, but she has "closed her spirit" to me. I've tried to get her to open her spirit to me consistently for the past two weeks, using some of the techniques in the videos, but I'm frustrated by how long this is taking. I've apologized, spoken softly and spoken from my heart, but this is taking an excruciatingly long time. She says that it took a long time to get her to this point and it's going to take a long time to get her head back where it was. This is really very hurtful for me since I now realize how important she is to me. Is there anything I can do to speed up this process?*

A: I (Gary) am so excited that you did not give up and that you are willing to give your marriage the nurture and time it needs. The keyword is time.

I have been married for more than 40 years. I love my wife more and more every day, but there are days when Norma has a closed spirit toward me. We still must work at our marriage every day. That's what makes marriage so exciting: It is a work in progress. Even in my 60s, God is still working on me. He's not done with me yet.

Two keys to your success strike me as I read your email. First, "speeding up the process" implies that you have an end in mind and that once you achieve it, all will be perfect. Don't forget that you, your wife and your marriage are all works in progress. Change is typically slow and you must allow your wife time to heal and recover.

Second, take this time to work on yourself. What did you do to contribute to her closed spirit? Learn from that. What is God teaching you? Reflect on those lessons. Take a deep look on the inside and grow each day in the power of Christ.

Trying to speed up your wife's recovery will more than likely be counterproductive. Work on the only person you can change: you.

Blessings, my friend. Don't give up or lose heart.

Note
1. Beth Moore, *Get Out of That Pit: Straight Talk About God's Deliverance* (Nashville, TN: Thomas Nelson, 2007).

7

Deliver

Crafting the Perfect Apology

Amy has never been impressed with my trite apologies, which can come across as though I were turning in an orange "Get out of jail free" card.

A perfunctory "I'm sorry" is not always enough.

The year before our first child was born, Amy and I planted a church in Branson, Missouri. Getting a church off the ground required a ton of time and two tons of energy. We spent 60 to 80 hours a week working. We never complained about the work because it was, and continues to be, our passion. It was an overflow of our life and consumed our conversations, trips to the store and evening laptop time. There was always something to be done. And when you are the only two staff members of a 500-member church, it's on you to "git 'er done."

During the early years of church planting, we became very close to our small group. We spent time each week with a number of young couples that shared our season of life. Some had children and some did not.

When we announced to our group that we were expecting, I said something that made sense to me but I had no idea how badly it would hurt Amy. The result and fallout from those ill-chosen words would change our marriage forever. More importantly, it changed me forever.

"Nothing is going to change once the baby is born," I declared to our small group. My words were not intended to hurt; it was simply my attempt to assure everyone that we would continue leading the church with all of our time and energy.

Amy heard it in a completely different way, and it rocked her world. She heard, "We are still going to work long hours each week. We will still go out to dinner regularly with friends. We will put in long nights at church. Don't expect our lives or schedules to be any different." Nothing could have been further from the reality that would soon engulf our lives.

In our marriage conferences that we hold around the country, we teach that communication is more about what the other person is hearing than the words you are saying. Feelings are more important than words. A woman's intuition is like Superman's X-ray vision into the heart. Amy saw my heart when I spoke the words "Nothing will change." She knew that I was not prepared for reality. I had making a baby all figured out. That part was fun. And the classes prepared me for the labor and delivery. However, I was not ready to be a dad. It would take me years to figure it all out. Balancing marriage, career and parenting would prove to be the greatest challenge of my life.

After my small-group announcement, later that night Amy shared with me, "Ted, I hope you know that things *are* going to change." Well, hold on for a shocker, but that started a pretty huge fight. I blew up, wanting her to stay focused on what we were called to do and just add a precious baby to the mix. I was such a jerk. I was focused on finding a solution rather than on connecting. I know better now. Connecting is more important than solving. Our frustration directed toward one another grew over the next few days, and there was much silence around our home.

I wanted to protect my self-interests. The more Amy realized this, the worse it got. What I didn't realize was that Amy was not telling me to stop being a pastor; she wanted to know that I valued her and the new life that God was blessing us with. Once I realized those were her thoughts, things started to change.

I sat her down one night and went way beyond "I'm sorry." I needed her to know what I had discovered and what I was sorry for. Through tears, I apologized for (1) being a jerk; (2) not valuing her; and (3) an overwhelming lack of consideration for the future of our family. My wife forgave, as she always does.

I learned not to wait days for something that can be resolved today. I learned to identify when my "I'm sorry" was genuine and not say it until that moment. I learned that authentic apologies are not for the weak-hearted. It takes guts. I learned that vulnerability models a behavior that others will want to follow.

How many times have you offered a genuine, authentic apology and then your mate responds with the same? That is the secret test. If your apology is met with resistance or a closed posture, most of the time, but not always, it is a sign of something still missing from the apology. As Scripture says, "A word aptly spoken is like apples of gold in settings of silver" (Prov. 25:11).

All too often we're tempted to take shortcuts when it comes to offering an apology—particularly to our spouse. We rely on half-hearted phrases such as "Sorry" and "I didn't mean to" to get us off the hook. A real apology, on the other hand, establishes a foundation for reconciliation not only in the moment but for the future.

That's why we want to give you five tools to help you craft sincere, authentic apologies and explore the attitude that will make all the difference when you deliver them.

Five Tools to Craft the Best Apology

When something goes wrong in a relationship, there's so much that can be said and so much that shouldn't be said. The tools in this section can help you craft an authentic and appropriate apology no matter what your situation.

Tool 1: Put Some Thought into It

Before you open your mouth, spend some time thinking about what you're going to say. I highly recommend taking at least 15 minutes, if not more, to think things through.

A flippant or insincere apology
can do more damage than good.

A few minutes of thoughtful reflection will also help connect your heart to your words. If I do something foolish or selfish in my relationship with Amy, and then I apologize in less than 90 seconds, my wife knows that I haven't thought it through. My apology isn't really sincere. A flippant or insincere apology can do more damage than good. We all need to take the time to think about what we've done before we apologize. The Bible says, "There is more hope for a fool than for someone who speaks without thinking" (Prov. 29:20, *NLT*).

Recently, Amy and I were at Build-a-Bear and got snippy with each other. We exchanged words. We had driven separately, and as we pulled out of the mall parking lot, I took a few moments to reflect on my attitude and reaction. (Notice that I focused on *my* part and left her part between her and God. As much as I would have liked to rehearse her faults, I resisted those thoughts and stuck to what *I* did or didn't do that offended her.) After reviewing my part in our squabble, I decided to call Amy on the cell phone: "I'm sorry, honey. Would you forgive me for snapping at you in Build-A-Bear? I apologize for being disconnected from you."

I know that my wife's hot button issue is feeling disconnected. Taking time to reflect and add those few words made all the difference.

She said, "I forgive you! Will you forgive me too?" By the time we arrived home, we were reconnected again.

The next time you find yourself crafting an apology, take time to put the appropriate amount of thought into it.

Tool 2: Focus on Feelings, Not Issues

Compassion is placing someone else's hurt feelings into your own heart. While it's easy to focus on the issue at hand, it's more important to focus on the feelings when it comes to crafting an apology.

No matter what has happened, there are always two sides to every story. Put yourself in your spouse's shoes. See if you can understand his or her pain and hurt. You may need to apologize: "I am sorry for giving you the idea that I was abandoning you" or "I am sorry for rejecting you." Then repeat the words you said to cause pain and let your spouse know that you shouldn't have said those things.

We like to hide behind money, sex, kids and jobs,
but the issue is never the issue.

We like to hide behind money, sex, kids and jobs, but the issue is never the issue. For example, a couple may have conflict over the husband's tardiness night after night. But they make a mistake if they focus on the issue of his tardiness, because there is no right or wrong time for being home at night. The spouse who comes home at 5:00 P.M. is no better than the spouse who comes home at 6:00 P.M. The issue is not the time, so they should focus on feelings.

"You said you would be home at five o' clock."

"I know, but things came up."

"Why didn't you call?"

Ah-ha! The issue is not about the hour on the clock but the desire for a telephone call, a sign of respect and courtesy.

"Sorry I didn't call!"

"Yeah, that's what you always say."

Notice that the *real* issues are starting to come out. The wife is acknowledging a pattern of behavior. *You love your job more than me*, she thinks, without verbalizing.

Unfortunately, most couples end the discussion right there. The husband leaves the conversation, thinking that the issue is about work, phone calls and tardiness; but the wife is actually feeling disrespected, worthless, unwanted and invalidated.

Remember our chapter on key buttons that get pushed? Always search for the emotions that point to core fears and commit not to build a case against the other person. Arguing over issues can lead to escalation of emotional reaction; but listening for your spouse's core fears is what brings the discussion to a quick resolution.

When spouses can dig deep into each other's hearts, then real healing can begin. An apology that speaks to a spouse's feelings can bring restoration.

"I'm sorry for coming home late. My job is not more important than you."

"I'm sorry for being late. I should have called to connect and let you know where I was."

"You deserve better than that, babe . . . I'm sorry."

No matter the topic of disagreement in your marriage, remember that it's not about winning or losing. The apostle Paul realized this when he encountered a hot-button issue in the Corinthian church: whether or not to eat meat sacrificed to idols (see 1 Cor. 8). Some believers were concerned that meat sacrificed on the altars of pagan gods might taint them spiritually. Others, including Paul, believed that meat was not a spiritual issue, and eating it was permissible. However, Paul said, understanding one another's position was more important than eating or not eating the meat. Working to understand the issue from another's point of view shows honor and respect.

Work at listening to what your spouse is saying, not just to the words he or she uses. When your spouse sees and senses that you are listening, he or she feels valued. True listening is obvious. You show your spouse that you are listening through your body language, your nonverbal responses (such as facial expressions and eye contact) and by asking questions. Furthermore, you focus your attention on your spouse and pick up on nonverbal cues or signals he or she is giving you.

The point of listening is to understand
the other person.

Listening does not require that you solve problems; the point of listening is to understand the other person, and good listening takes time (that's why so few people practice it, much less master it). The degree to which someone feels listened to is the degree to which he or she will grant you opportunities to communicate your feelings. Who wants to talk to someone who doesn't listen? For that matter, who wants to live with someone who doesn't listen?

When you find yourself disagreeing with your spouse, what steps can you take to become a better listener? Try saying, "Let me see if I'm hearing you right" or "What I hear you saying is . . ." and repeating back what you've just heard your spouse say. Then ask, "Do you think I'm understanding you?"

What Amy and I have found when we focus on feelings instead of issues is that the issues just seem to fall away. So long as we are both deeply understood by each other, it doesn't really matter what we decide on a particular issue. For example, for a long time money was a source of anger and tension in our marriage. Amy grew up in a home that defined savings as the difference between the list price and the sale price. The home I grew up in defined savings as the money you put away for a rainy day.

For the first seven or eight years of our marriage, Amy was the spender and I was the saver. We fought all the time about money. But for the past four years, as we have focused on each other's heart instead of our own opinions, our marriage has flipped upside down: I am the spender and she is the saver.

What?! Why?

Better than trying to explain it, I challenge you to try it. During your next fight or heated discussion, ask this set of questions:

- How did your parents handle these situations when you were growing up?
- If we go with this decision, what will be your greatest fear?
- What thrills you the most about this decision?
- Do you feel like a winner or a loser with this decision?
- What would make you feel like a winner?

Questions like these are a win-win ending to every argument. (What a great goal!) A winning solution goes beyond merely finding what is acceptable or tolerable to you both. That's compromise, which rarely makes anyone feel good. Redefine winning as *finding and implementing a solution that both people can feel good about.*

At this point, you may be asking, "What about the 'right or wrong' issues? Black or white issues? Absolute truth?" We are not talking here about the foundations of our faith—most of the issues we fight about fall under the "it could go either way" category. Be careful not to place God on your side in these conversations as an opponent of your mate.

Tool 3: Become a Great Wordsmith

When it comes to crafting a great apology, it helps to expand your vocabulary. If you don't already own one, buy a dictionary. If you have a computer with Internet access, bookmark two sites: www.dictionary.com and www.thesaurus.com.

I reached the end of my apologetic vocabulary very early in my marriage to Amy. When we had a fight, I ended the conflict by saying a single word: "Sorry." I used it a lot. In fact, I think I used it up in the first few months of marriage!

When you use the same words repeatedly
with your spouse, sooner or later
they will come off as insincere.

Now I constantly look for new ways to craft an apology. I keep a dictionary on my desk and try to learn a new word every couple of days. This helps keep my vocabulary fresh and gives me new ways to express my thoughts and feelings. When you use the same words repeatedly with your spouse, sooner or later they can come off as insincere. To avoid such ruts, keep adding to your vocabulary.

The Bible says, "Pleasant words are a honeycomb, sweet to the soul and healing to the bones. . . . Reckless words pierce like a sword, but the tongue of the wise brings healing" (Prov. 16:24; 12:18). When you put some thought into it, focus on feelings instead of on issues; and become a great wordsmith, your words will be like honeycomb and bring healing and restoration. You will be amazed at how quickly taking ownership over an issue or character defect can melt the heart of your spouse. Find fresh ways to take responsibility:

- "You deserve a medal just living with me."
- "You're way too valuable to treat like this."
- "I was so wrong to say those things to you."

- "I am going to let my actions say that I am sorry."
- "Will you forgive me?"
- "I know why I just did that, and it was wrong."
- "It is my fault."
- "I take 100-percent responsibility for how bad that conversation just went."
- "This is my issue and something I need to work on."
- "That is a character defect in me that I will ask God to help me with."

Think about this apology: "I'm sorry you were hurt." What do these words mean? Are you saying the person shouldn't have been hurt? Are you saying their hurt wasn't really justified? Someone can read a lot of things into those reckless words. Or consider this one: "I'm sorry if I offended you." Those words express no ownership of the part you played in your spouse's pain, and the words are so vague that your spouse may wonder what you mean.

"I'm sorry if I offended you." Those words
express no ownership of the part you played
in your spouse's pain.

Your spouse may feel hurt because he or she is immature or childish, but it really doesn't matter: Love cares for others unconditionally. It's hard to love like God, so don't try to. Instead, let God give you His love as you seek Him day and night. Become the branch that stays grafted to the Vine and wait for His love to flow into and out of you. You'll catch yourself feeling grieved when others hurt because of your actions.

As I have practiced this, I am sensitive when I cause pain to others. I do not want others to feel pain because of my actions, period. If they are hurt because of me, I want to do my part to repair the wrong.

Ask your spouse to give you examples of a well-crafted apology and a reckless apology. Ask what words or phrases come across as insincere to him or her. You might be surprised at what you discover! Words are much like toothpaste squeezed from the tube: You can never put them back inside your mouth once they are spoken. So become a great wordsmith and allow your words to be sweet like honeycomb to your spouse.

Tool 4: Remember that Less Is More

Have you ever had someone apologize and then go historical on you? They bring up issues and events from 10 months or even 10 years ago. By the end of the apology, you're more upset than when the person began. During those encounters, you have the opportunity to extend grace and appreciate the fact that he or she made an effort. You also have an opportunity to learn from the person's mistake.

A well-crafted apology is short and to the point. You don't need to offer a dissertation on the situation. Apologize, state the offense and then take ownership of the hurt you've caused. Let your spouse know that you never meant to push his or her buttons in that way. The Bible advises, "Fire goes out for lack of fuel" (Prov. 26:20, *NLT*). A concise, well-crafted apology doesn't add fuel to the fire and brings a quick end to dispute.

If necessary, write down your apology before you say it aloud, or share it with someone else for the purpose of accountability. I (Gary) remember working for a very strong Christian leader who sincerely wanted to reestablish harmony with a person he had offended. But each time he tried to apologize, he brought up what the other person had done and scolded the person for his poor reaction to his words and actions. The offended person was always disappointed, and healing could not take place.

A great wordsmith finds the right words, uses less of them and puts some thought into them. Above all, avoid playing the historian and bringing up every offense possible.

Tool 5: Apologize in Person

Unless extreme circumstances prevent it, always apologize face to face. Neither email nor handwritten letters come close to an in-person apology. If you have to send a letter or an email to someone, make sure that two or three people read it before you send it out. Let them be a second and third set of eyes to ensure that your words are coming from a place of grace, love and restoration. Make sure the words you're communicating are like honeycomb, not like a sword that pierces the soul.

You need to apologize with your facial expression and body language as much, if not more, than with your words.

I've messed up in this area countless times. I now have a steadfast rule about confronting or apologizing in written form: If at all possible, I just don't do it. I try never to send out an email to anyone when I have something important to say—especially if I'm seeking forgiveness—but there are times when it's unavoidable. When it can't be helped, I always have my wife read the apology before I send it out, and sometimes another trusted friend or family member. A second or third pair of eyes reviewing my words can make all the difference in a well-crafted apology.

The Secret of a Perfect Apology

Even if you put some thought into it, you focus on feelings more than what is said, you use meaningful words and you deliver a textbook perfect apology, your apology will still not be the best it can be without one essential element: *gentleness.*

With just one or two sentences that are calm rather than mean, degrading or belittling, you can reduce the threat level in a situation and extinguish anger.

The word "gentleness" appears almost two dozen times in the Bible. "Gentle" is the word used to describe Jesus as He rode into Jerusalem for His triumphal entry (see Matt. 21:5). In defense of his own ministry, the apostle Paul said,

"By the meekness and gentleness of Christ, I appeal to you" (2 Cor. 10:1). Gentleness is also listed as one of the fruit of the spirit (see Gal. 5:23).

The word "gentle" may not be a familiar one in your vocabulary, but as a follower of Jesus, you need to encourage it in others and yourself. Always lace your apologies with gentleness. Proverbs 15:1 says, "A gentle answer turns away wrath, but a harsh word stirs up anger." This means that no matter what situation you're in and no matter what has been said or done to you, a gentle response is the best response. With just one or two sentences that are calm rather than mean, degrading or belittling, you can reduce the threat level in a situation and extinguish anger. When an apology is delivered with gentleness, you'll be amazed at the results.

Throughout this book, I (Ted) have shared with you the story of my near-firing from my first pastorate. The principles Gary used to mentor me through that time are what are presented in this book. As Paul Harvey says, "Now, the rest of the story."

The founding pastor of the church that almost fired me faithfully pastored there for five years. Through a series of unfortunate struggles and conflicts, he left the church a year prior to my arrival. I became senior pastor in the spring of 2001, long on schooling and short on experience.

As the events I've already described unfolded, I realized that my time there was limited. I eventually departed in much more harmony with the congregation than I expected and planted a church in Branson with a small group of loving and loyal friends. It's important to mention that I did not negotiate my exit on my own. I consulted counselors and a host of loving, wise and godly people to help me and help the church through the transition.

Shortly after the other pastors expressed their feelings that I was not the guy for the church, the founding pastor was mentioned as a possibility for my replacement, thus making him both my predecessor and my successor.

Fast-forward six years. I am now gone from that church and am the senior pastor of Woodland Hills Community Church in Branson, Missouri. The founding pastor was again the senior pastor of the other church and was serving as a board member and speaker for NIM (The National Institute of Marriage), which was founded by Gary Smalley. In August 2006, I was scheduled to speak at an NIM conference in Toledo, Ohio. Bob Paul, co-president of NIM and a close friend, called to tell me that he had decided to have this pastor speak with me in Toledo.

Acting all mature on the phone, I said, "No problem." Inside, I was dying.

That night, I told Amy, "I have been doing my own thing for five-plus years now. I leave them alone; they leave me alone. I have gone five years without communicating with them. Why start now? [This would be a good place for me to remind you that I am a *pastor*.] Amy, I really don't need this. Bob can do the conference without me."

"Do you really think that is best?" Amy asked. (A year later, Amy admitted that she struggled with the assignment as well.)

I kept the conference on my schedule. The flight to Toledo worked out well because I was in seat 16C and my predecessor/successor was in 18C. We were not seated together. Then we made it through the weekend seminar with few words spoken. I can't begin to tell you how much I felt like I was dodging a bullet.

Then my luck ran out. The flight from Toledo to Chicago was empty. We sat across the aisle from each other, and there was a humongous "pink elephant" swinging his trunk right between us. We survived the flight by talking around the elephant. A few awkward moments were interrupted by a flight attendant. God bless that woman.

However, there was no escaping O'Hare Airport, gate K3. Cursed be that gate. When the elephant could no longer be ignored, my successor (being older and wiser) looked at me and said, "I hate that you and Amy had to go through all that you went through. I'm sorry." This was the first acknowledgment of all that I had endured, and those 17 words changed my life forever. They set me free in ways I had hoped for, prayed for and waited for. There was so much emotional energy I had stored up over the years, but it only took 17 words to drain the entire vat of discouragement from my heart.

"I'm sorry too," I said, and it was done. The elephant died and fell to the floor as if it had been filled with nothing but air. It had no chance against two sincere apologies.

That one encounter makes me want to see more of God's children reconciled and set free. Sometimes all it takes is 17 words or less.

I see that pastor every now and then on the streets of Branson, and it is as though nothing ever happened. I am comfortable and free to encourage him with all he is doing for God. We each agree that *both* churches need to be successful to bring glory to God.

A well-crafted, sincere apology is one of the most powerful tools you can use in your marriage (and any other relationship). In the next chapter, we look at nine roadblocks that can stand in the way of offering a meaningful apology and real forgiveness. We'll teach you how to develop your own forgiveness list and move into levels of freedom and restoration that you've never experienced before.

From GarySmalley.com

Q: *I've really been struggling in one of my relationships and I don't know how to handle it. What do you do when someone keeps apologizing but isn't sincere?*

A: The sincerity of an apology is validated by behavior. If behavior does not change, that invalidates the apology. Sometimes we just say the words to get us off the hook. We want to just get out of the fight and be done with it.

I (Ted) tend to withdraw. When things go bad, I go to the basement. Sometimes before I withdraw, I stir things up a little bit, which then starts Amy's emotions escalating. Then I think, *If she is going to talk to me that way, I am out of here,* even though I was the one that brought all of this fuel and venom into the fight. But instead of admitting my fault and changing my ways, I say "I'm sorry" to just get it over with, to make her happy again. I use "I'm sorry" to restore momentary peace to the home. Apologies are insincere when they are not followed by a change of behavior.

The sincerity of the apology cannot determine whether or not you forgive. The act of forgiveness is the only answer—sincere apology or not. Don't consume your energy worrying about what your loved one did to you. You are not in control of him (or her), and thus you can't make him seek forgiveness or accept your forgiveness. You can only control your own life and how you behave. However, the proven sincerity of the apology does determine the boundaries you set for the future.

Be careful not to confuse forgiveness with accepting or condoning what someone did to you. You might think, *If I forgive my assailant, then what he did is excused!* It is important to understand that forgiveness has nothing to do with "condoning" someone's actions against you. Real forgiveness has everything to do with freeing yourself to move beyond the offense and gain new and more refined strength and stability only available through God's grace.

It doesn't help a relationship—it doesn't help it in the least—to focus on all the stuff you think the other person needs to change. Don't allow your forgiveness to become a tool for the other person's behavior modification. Let God alone change the person, because you can't. Address what you are doing, look at your own thoughts and reactions, and ponder your own emotions. It does help when you do your own personal work.

8

Relent

Overturning Roadblocks to Forgiveness

I (Ted) have always viewed "Do not enter" signs as challenges. *What don't they want me to see?* I ask myself. Curiosity always gets the best of me.

Several winters ago, a major ice storm hit the hills of the Ozarks. Almost every street and business was shut down for days. The road behind our church office is one of the steepest in Branson, and ice seems to stick longer there than on any other road. Despite this fact, when I was out driving a few days later, I decided to try to see if I could make it up the hill. The roadblock sign that was posted on the road was as plain as day, but I told Amy, "They have just not had time to get the sign removed. I know I can make it."

Half way up the hill, my confidence was waning. Three quarters the way up, our tires started spinning, and we could not reach the peak. We were in a predicament. I was embarrassed.

Once I knew that we were stuck, I immediately turned to Amy and said, "I'm sorry."

She rolled her eyes. "What are you going to do now," she asked.

"Hug the curb and creep back down the hill," I said, sighing sheepishly. After all, I could not sit there for days waiting for the ice to melt.

"There is a reason the roadblock sign was there," she patiently stated. "You can't go around it."

We all have roadblocks to forgiveness in our marriages. Let's look at some ways to remove them and keep from going around them.

Nine Roadblocks to Forgiveness

The idea of forgiving someone may be overwhelming to you. You may have lived with anger your whole life. You may look back and see lines of people who have offended you or whom you have offended. Whether you see a handful of people, a small crowd or a large gathering in your mind, you can move forward into forgiveness. But you will only be able to move forward as far as you clean up behind yourself.

In this chapter we look at the nine roadblocks to forgiveness and give you tactics for how to clear them out of your life. We also ask you to look at the final 15 minutes of your life and develop a forgiveness list. This is an exercise that has the potential to change your life and relationships forever.

First, let's look at nine roadblocks to forgiveness.

Roadblock 1: Selfishness

The first roadblock to forgiveness is selfishness. James 4:1 asks, "What causes fights and quarrels among you? Don't they come from your desires that battle within you?" It's easy to look at someone else as both the problem and the solution; but when you do that, you are stuck. You're held hostage by the circumstances. There's nowhere for you to go. You may have made the mistake of thinking that cutting off a relationship in your life will change everything, but the deep truth is that wherever you go, that person is in your mind. You take all of your past hurts and victories with you wherever you move. You are the common denominator in your relationships, so if you haven't already begun, it's time to begin taking personal responsibility for every one.

*You are the common denominator
in your relationships.*

Serving is the antidote for selfishness. Serving others is simply giving something away and expecting nothing in return. You wouldn't believe the freedom you will experience when you bless someone who has wronged you. Resentment, grumbling and outright anger toward that person cannot coexist in a heart that wishes the best for the person. Give without expecting anything in return, then watch how doing so transforms you—your attitude, your reactions and, ultimately, the intimacy of your relationships.

Roadblock 2: Pride
The Bible says that God opposes the proud; He actually stands against those who are prideful (see Prov. 3:34). On the flip side, James 4:6 says that He gives grace to the

humble. How do you increase your humility? By recognizing that everything you have and everything you are comes from God. Nothing is of your own work; you cannot do anything on your own. The antidote to pride is dependence on God.

Humility also means being transparent. We are convinced that the number-one fear most people suffer is being found out. Proverbs 16:18 says, "Pride will destroy a person: a proud attitude leads to ruin" (*NCV*). Many of us have been in a relationship in which someone found out something about us and it led to their rejection of us; but we can't move forward if we're driven by the need to protect ourselves. Humility lays the soul bare in dependence on God.

Roadblock 3: Insecurity

Insecurity keeps us from forgiving. We often get emails from husbands who have told their wives for years that they need to lose weight, and from wives who belittle their husbands and make them feel like failures because they can't earn enough to support their family. Rather than bringing healing and restoration into their marriage, they sow seeds of doubt and hurt that only magnify personal insecurities.

If you have been told for years that you don't measure up, that you're a failure or that you're no good, those messages aren't just in your mind; they're in your heart. It will take weeks, months or longer of intensely bathing your mind, heart and soul in the truth of God's Word to free you from those lies. But it can be done. No matter what your insecurity, God wants you to find your security in Him. God invites you to fall in love with Him, to allow His words (the Bible) to penetrate your heart and your mind in order to transform you. Let Him whisper the truth into your heart that will set you free and revolutionize your marriage and any other relationship that needs healing.

Roadblock 4: Resentment

Have you ever tried to pull a bush out of the ground that has been planted there for years? If so, you know that it takes more than a shovel or a swift tug. A deep-rooted bush may require a chain towed by a truck to uproot it.

A few years ago, I (Ted) decided to plant a Bradford Pear tree in my yard. I thought it would be great if the kids could pick fresh fruit. A neighbor came by as I was digging the hole and asked what I was doing, so I explained my plan. He pointed out that if I planted the tree in the hole I had dug, within three years the roots would begin to eat into the foundation of our house. I was grateful for his wise words, and I've never forgotten that lesson in gardening, and as it applies to life.

God instructs us to be careful not to allow the roots of resentment to grow in our life.

When seeds of resentment and bitterness are planted in our soul and given time to grow, their roots run deep. It can take a chain and a truck to remove them. That's why God instructs us to be careful not to allow the roots of resentment to grow in our life. If we do allow them to grow, before we know it, those roots will undermine our foundation and cloud our perspective. The psalmist experienced this when he wrote, "Since my heart was embittered and my soul deeply wounded [this is what bitterness does], I was stupid and could not understand" (Ps. 73:21-22, *NAB*). Not only does resentment hurt you, but it will hurt those around you. The writer of Hebrews notes, "For as it springs up it causes deep trouble, hurting many in their spiritual lives" (Heb. 12:15, *TLB*).

Fortunately, there is an antidote for the presence of resentment: the antidote is forgiveness. Forgiving—letting go—allows you to pull out the deepest roots of anger and resentment. Just as God forgives you, you are to forgive others. Colossians 3:13 instructs, "You must make allowance for each other's faults and forgive the person who offended you. Remember the Lord forgave you, so you must forgive others" (*NLT*). Notice that the Bible says "you *must*." Forgiveness isn't optional. You need to forgive just as much as the person who has hurt you needs to be forgiven. When it comes to forgiveness, we're all on equal footing.

As we said in the previous chapter, it is much easier to forgive others when we realize what God has forgiven us. Make a list of the worst sins that you have committed during your life. Destroy it, but not before you take time to see that God buries your sin in the deepest sea when you confess it.

Occasionally, it crosses my mind that when we get to heaven, all of my family and friends will see the sins I committed during my lifetime. Then I relax and remember that when I confess my sins, not only does God forgive me, but He buries them in the deepest sea, never to be remembered again. And just as important, the more of God's key words I hide within my heart, the less and less I sin against Him (see Ps. 119:11).

Roadblock 5: Unresolved Anger

We've discussed the issue of unresolved anger throughout the book, but it is still one of the key roadblocks to forgiveness. Unresolved anger is a poison we drink. Our secret hope when we drink this poison is that the other person will get sick; but we're the ones who become ill, dying from the inside out with bitterness, envy and malice. Don't allow unresolved anger to hold you back from who you're called (and created) to be. When you resolve your anger and seek forgiveness, not only do you set the other person free, but you also get free.

Roadblock 6: Inability to Recognize Your Weaknesses and Mistakes

It's easy to find fault with someone else, but when you choose to play the role of the critic, you set up your own roadblock to forgiveness. Before you know it, you become so focused on someone else's weaknesses and mistakes that you cannot see your own. In the process, you refuse personal responsibility. You look at the chinks in someone else's armor and spend your time and energy exposing them to others. Remember our discussion about seeing the "speck" in your spouse's eye when you've got a giant "log" sticking out from yours? This kind of behavior and mindset is a major roadblock to forgiveness.

If you have difficulty seeing your own sins or mistakes and find yourself focusing instead on the sins of others, you may be heading down the road to narcissism. Matthew 7 warns not to judge your neighbor, because you will be judged in the same way. You have to deal with your own issues and struggles before you can help anyone else. In the process of facing your own weakness, you become a little less judgmental and a little more loving toward others. (My favorite book that exposes the extreme self-centered person is *People of the Lie* by M. Scott Peck. It explains how to help those who are locked into a self-focused lifestyle.)

The truth is that any time the other person is both the problem and the solution, we get stuck.

One of the reasons forgiveness is so hard is because when we find ourselves in conflict, it's easy to think the other person has all the problems. The truth is that any time the other person is both the problem and the solution, we get stuck. If your spouse is the problem *and* the solution, there's no place to go. That's why you have to take a good, hard look at yourself and the areas you need to work on in order to move toward forgiveness.

I (Gary) easily admit today that when I was first married, I truly could not see my faults. Norma's, however, were very clear in my mind. I tried and tried to change her, because I believed that if she changed, I could be happier. Now I only work on myself. The more I reflect deeply on who I am and who I am becoming, the easier it is to call on God and His words in Scripture to reform me. And the more that Norma sees me change, I've noticed that her own desire to become more like Christ increases. I've stopped being the Holy Spirit for her and have released her to work on her own relationship with God.

Roadblock 7: Misunderstanding Forgiveness

Forgiveness is like pushing a release button. You let the other person go. Unfortunately, there are a lot of misperceptions of forgiveness. Some people buy into the myth that to truly forgive, you must "forgive and forget." They believe that if you still remember the offense, you haven't honestly forgiven. But as followers of Jesus Christ, we are invited to forgive even when we remember the offense committed against us. We don't have to forget in order to forgive. When you push the release button of forgiveness, however, you give up your right to bring up the issue again and make the other person feel bad about what he or she has done.

Why do so many people remind their offender of past wrongs committed? Because they would like to change the offender so that he or she never offends them in the same way again. But two of the greatest lies on this earth are:

1. If I can change the other person, or if they'll stop hurting me, I will be happier.

2. If I can change my circumstances (more money, bigger house, nicer car), I will be happier.

These two lies are so destructive because they take the focus off of the changes that need to happen in our own life—the only changes that truly lead to our freedom and satisfaction. I am learning that I am only as happy as the beliefs I store in my heart. Jesus told us that our thoughts, words and actions flow out of our heart (see Matt. 15:19-20). And because our emotions are simply data that tell us what we have been thinking, saying and doing, our beliefs are just about all there is about us. I've been learning with great delight that as I change my beliefs to match those of Christ and His words, I am freer and happier than I have been at any other time in my life. It's so much easier for me to forgive others, because their actions toward me cannot affect my beliefs. My new beliefs shield me from the "barbs" of others.[1]

You may have asked God to forgive you but haven't yet accepted the forgiveness He offers, so you keep replaying the situation in your mind.

It's also important to remember that the person you have the hardest time forgiving may be yourself. You may be holding something against yourself that you did 10 or 20 years ago. You may have asked God to forgive you but haven't yet accepted the forgiveness He offers, so you keep replaying the situation in your mind. Rest assured that God's promise of forgiveness to those who ask is 100-percent true. He is totally trustworthy. When you accept His forgiveness for yourself, you will be empowered to extend it to countless others.

Roadblock 8: Fear of Condoning the Offense

In the process of building our house a few years ago, I (Ted) lost my cool with a guy in town over a customer service issue. I had gotten in the car to drive away when I remembered that we were in the middle of a series on serving at our church.

I knew I had to walk back into this man's business and apologize to him. Now, there's nothing worse than having to apologize to a condescending person. My lip started quivering as I said, "I need to apologize to you for snapping at you earlier." But when he accepted, I felt as if a weight had been lifted off of me. I couldn't tell if it made any difference in the man's life, but it made a big one in mine.

---

*Your marriage doesn't need both of you
to make a change in this moment—just one
of you needs to make a change.*

After a few minutes of conversation, I said, "I want to be clear here that I am not overlooking the mishaps in the house construction. Those still need to be resolved.

I'm apologizing for my tone and attitude. For those, I'm sorry."

You can offer forgiveness without condoning an offense. Often when I'm counseling couples in conflict, I remind them, "Only one of you has to make the right move here. Your marriage doesn't need both of you to make a change in this moment—just one of you needs to make a change." Over time, the change will be seen and appreciated and has the power to transform the relationship.

We see this all the time in the Marriage Intensives at the National Institute of Marriage. One spouse breaks and is humbled before God. When one spouse admits his or her mistakes and takes personal responsibility, it changes everything. You can begin today to turn your marriage around. Don't wait for your spouse to change. Change yourself.

Roadblock 9: The Passage of Time

You've probably heard it said that time heals all wounds. But it's not a verse in the Bible, and it's simply not true. You may be tempted to think that because something happened years ago, it's not relevant today. Yet if the right situation or circumstance arises, the past hurt will be the first thing on your mind.

No matter how much time has passed since an offense, you need to take steps to resolve it. You may need to sit down and have a face-to-face conversation after crafting a sincere and meaningful apology. You may need to write someone a letter if you can't see him (or her). You may need to have a good heart-to-heart with God about what happened. Don't allow time to stand in your way. Clear out the roadblock so that you can give and experience forgiveness in your life.

The nine roadblocks to forgiveness do not hinder only one particular relationship in your life; they hinder *all* of your relationships. You see, the belief you carry in your heart about one person is a belief you quietly carry into every relationship.

Only Fifteen Minutes to Live

Amy and I had our first emergency landing in an airplane on our eleventh anniversary. It might be a stretch to call it a near-death experience, but the conversation that flowed between us during the crisis showed us the truth of James 4:14: "What is your life? You are a mist that appears for a little while and then vanishes."

When the jetway to our plane turned out to be a stairwell, I knew we were headed to a small plane. What I wasn't prepared for was a winged aircraft that looked like a leftover from the 1950s. The once-bright white paint had faded to a pale, worn yellow; stepping onboard the dated, cramped cabin made me feel less than comfortable. Amy looked at me and said, "Does this plane look safe to you?"

I responded like a good husband: "A major airline would not allow a plane in service unless it was completely safe and proven." Secretly, I had my doubts.

About halfway through the short flight from Atlanta to Asheville, the pilot announced, "We want to make you aware of a little situation, but we don't want you to worry." (Now that's the kind of statement that immediately makes everyone want to worry!) The pilot went on to explain that there was a problem with the flaps on the wings. The problem was that they weren't working. Because the runway in Asheville wasn't long enough to accommodate the situation, we were returning to Atlanta.

We all felt relieved. After all, turning around an aircraft wasn't a big deal. Or so we thought until a few minutes later when the pilot announced, "We don't want you to be alarmed, but our aircraft will be met by airport emergency personnel."

I leaned over to Amy and gently whispered, "I've had a great 11 years with you."

"None of that," she protested. "We're going to be just fine."

I started singing her a few lines from Tim McGraw's award-winning song "Live Like You Were Dying."

She rolled her eyes and said, "You are so dramatic."

"Seriously, Amy, I have absolutely no regrets! I just upped my life insurance to a good amount. The kids will be taken care of. I have no words unspoken that I wish I'd said to someone. I have no relationship that needs to be mended. I am ready if the Lord wants to take me."

For the final 15 minutes of that flight, Amy and I enjoyed a sweet time together. We spoke as if it were our last 15 minutes together on Earth.

When the pilot finally landed, there were nearly a dozen emergency vehicles waiting for us. The captain did a beautiful job, and everyone on board was glad to be safely on the ground.

Yet, within just a few minutes of one of the sweetest, richest conversations of our marriage, I immediately went back to being the old Ted. I complained to Amy, "Great, now we're going to be late to the conference. We'll probably have to drive. They ought to get us another plane ASAP. Since we're the first ones off, I'll run ahead of everybody to get a seat on a later flight."

I believe that we should live every minute of every day as if it were our last—filled with passion and purpose.

It's amazing how quickly we can remove ourselves from the mode of live-like-you-were-dying. But still, I challenge you to try it. I believe that we should live every minute of every day as if it were our last—filled with passion and purpose. It is down that road that we find true significance.

So, imagine yourself in your final 15 minutes. Who would you talk to if you knew you had only 15 minutes to live? Who would you need to forgive? From whom would you need to ask forgiveness?

Chances are good that you have more than 15 minutes to live. So what do you need to do in the upcoming days and weeks to find the sweet spot in your relationship with your mate, and in any other relationship that needs to be renewed through forgiveness?

The Forgiveness List

Now that you can recognize and remove the roadblocks, and recognize how you would spend your final 15 minutes on earth, it's time to put forgiveness into practice. Begin by making a list of people who have offended you, hurt you or let you down. You may think of teachers, coaches, pastors, leaders, parents, family members, friends, bosses, coworkers, neighbors or even people you've observed from a distance. Quietly ask God to speak to your heart and begin to reveal who belongs on your list. You'll be amazed at how many names begin to surface.

Over the next week, pay attention to your actions and reactions. Is there anyone in the grocery store that you try to avoid? Are you tempted to duck your head so that you don't have to get into a conversation with someone at a restaurant? Do you see a number on your caller ID and decide not to pick up because of an unresolved issue? The indicators are usually subtle, but they are signs of unforgiveness.

Just recently I was in a movie theater when a couple I know walked in. Within 30 seconds, I had developed a quick exit strategy to leave when the movie was over so that I wouldn't have to talk to them. That was an indicator of my heart. I thought that I had no one left to clear things with, yet all of a sudden here was something I didn't want to let go. I had not forgiven them. I needed to take my issue to God in prayer and repentance and make things right.

Just because you haven't spoken to someone in years doesn't mean there is not a level of unforgiveness. You may harbor unforgiveness toward someone you see or work with every day. Seek reconciliation and forgiveness now. It will do you—and them—a world of good.

Over the next week, spend time in prayer forgiving each person. If possible, meet with each person one on one (or pick up the phone) to ask for forgiveness. If talking directly with the person is not a possibility, giving and receiving forgiveness can still happen.

One of my (Gary's) most important forgiveness times was when I sat in my office and went through every offense a certain person had done to me. I imagined Jesus sitting with the two of us on a bench. I recounted each offense out loud as Jesus put one arm around my shoulders and one around my offender's. I forgave, just as Jesus asked me to, with each confession from the other person. And Jesus helped me each time. He never let go of me with His arm, nor did He let go of the offender. He helped me for more than three hours. I was a limp rag by the time I couldn't think of any more offenses. Even then, I didn't feel free for about three weeks; but when the freedom finally came, I felt lighter than air. I was truly free. For most of those days during the three weeks, I thought, *Oh well, it didn't work for me.* But it did!

In the next chapter, we explore the four keys to forgiving a difficult spouse. Rest assured, no matter how impossible your marriage relationship may seem, it *is* possible to move into freedom and forgiveness with God's strength.

From GarySmalley.com

Q: *Do I have to forgive someone who hates me and doesn't care about my forgiveness? Do I have to forgive no matter what? Does this mean that I am a doormat to everyone who lives?*

A: As followers of Christ, we are called to love others—even those who are difficult to get along with—and avoid harboring unforgiveness, bitterness and unresolved anger. In Luke 6:27-28, Jesus said, "But I tell you who hear me: Love your enemies, do good to those who hate you, bless those who curse you, pray for those who mistreat you" (Luke 6:27-28). As He hung on the cross, He said, "Father, forgive them, for they do not know what they are doing" (Luke 23:34). Jesus was asking for forgiveness for people who did not ask for it. He showed a spirit of forgiveness.

According to Matthew 5:44-48, even our enemies are worthy of forgiveness:

> But I tell you: Love your enemies and pray for those who persecute you, that you may be sons of your Father in heaven. He causes his sun to rise on the evil and the good, and sends rain on the righteous and the unrighteous. If you love those who love you, what reward will you get? Are not even the tax collectors doing that? And if you greet only your brothers, what are you doing more than others? Do not even pagans do that? Be perfect [that is, mature], even as your heavenly Father is perfect.

This passage touches on the very nature of our merciful God, who is gracious to all. We are called to be perfect "as your heavenly Father is perfect." Even as we acknowledge that we cannot be completely perfect (mature) while existing on this planet, this verse calls us to strive for Christ's perfection, characterized by His willingness to love those who are unlovable and to forgive those who sin against Him. Why must we forgive? Because God knows how unresolved anger kills the spirit, and He gives this command to free us from eternal regret.

This does not mean that you have to be a doormat to those who have wronged you. You can forgive a dangerous person without remaining tied to him or her. For example, God does not expect you to stay in a house where your safety or the safety of your children is at stake. You can move out, protect your family and forgive all at the same time. It is not an either-or issue. But just as you protect and guard yourself from a dangerous relationship or situation, you need to guard your physical, emotional and spiritual health by not allowing unresolved anger to rule your life.

Note

1. In *Change Your Heart, Change Your Life*, you can read exactly what I do to change my beliefs.

9

Commit

Forgiving a Difficult Spouse

My (Gary's) wife, Norma, goes all out for holidays. Whether it's Fourth of July, Christmas, Easter or someone's birthday, she has boxes of decorations in our attic ready for the occasion. Celebrating and decorating are some of Norma's passions.

A few years ago, we were celebrating the Fourth of July at our house. Norma had been preparing for weeks, and the whole house was decorated in red, white and blue. The meats were marinating, ready for the grill. Vegetable trays were arranged and refrigerated. Desserts were freshly baked. Everything was in place for the 60 guests we anticipated on the following day.

We were sitting out on the back deck and I was talking with my daughter when she said, "Dad, we don't have any food in the house. Can we eat with you tonight?"

I didn't miss a beat: "Of course you can! The fridge is loaded. Mom has prepared a ton of food for our guests tomorrow. Bring the whole family."

As soon as I finished the invitation, I heard Norma clearing her throat loudly.

199

"What?" I asked.

"Gary, I don't think this is a great idea," she said.

Instantly, I felt tormented inside. She had pushed one of my main buttons: *She is controlling me!* I wanted to go after her and demand, *Whose house is this anyway?*

Instead, I took a breath and remembered the instruction of James 1:19: "Be quick to listen and slow to speak."

"Thank you, hon, for the reminder," I said, realizing that she wanted to save the preparations for tomorrow's celebration. "Why don't we all go out to dinner?" Everyone agreed and we enjoyed a relaxing time out as a family.

Now, in that moment—in a split second—I could have gotten into a major argument with my wife, right in front of my daughter and grandkids. I could have made a small issue into a defining issue, but through God's grace and wisdom, I chose to let it go.

These kinds of situations arise all too often in a marriage. One person speaks without thinking about all of the ramifications. A wife may say something that pushes a husband's button. The husband reacts by trying to change his wife because he doesn't like the feeling. That pushes her button. Now she's in pain and the argument is escalating. Things are becoming more and more difficult, and the pain from each spouse causes the argument to escalate out of control.

In this chapter we explain why one of the best things you can do for your marriage is treat your spouse like an enemy. Yes, you read that correctly! We will give you four keys to forgiving a difficult spouse.

Treat Your Spouse Like an Enemy

That last word wasn't a typo! As we explored in the last chapter, Jesus tells us to *love our enemies*. When Jesus instructs us to love our enemies in Luke 6:27, He is not talking about those people who irritate you at work or cut you off in traffic or talk too much in your book club. Those people may annoy you, but the person who can really wound you is the person you allow to get closest to you: your spouse.

What I've discovered is that when you talk about forgiveness, the first things most people bring up are exclusions to the command to forgive.

I get emails and letters about the issues of love and forgiveness more than any other topic. What I've discovered is that when you talk about forgiveness, the first things most people bring up are exclusions to the command to forgive. They may say they like the idea of forgiveness, or even believe in it, but then they're quick to ask, *What about in this case?* or *What if the person did such-and-such to me?*

I recently received a letter from a man who had been wounded in his relationships. He wrote:

What do you mean invest in people? I am tired of people. People are a pain in the [bleep]. *It seems that all I do is try to please everybody else and nobody is trying to please me. And, oh by the way, I am married. I believe that all women are self-agenda driven and they are very good at acting like that is not the case, especially Christian women. What a farce that is. They put on all these niceties and then stab you in the back. This is definitely a day and age of too much prosperity and I believe it has tarnished the Christian thinking and actions. If you don't agree with this, then you're really not accepted. I'm tired of us going around pursuing bigger houses and faster cars. It is all vanity.*

He has cut out the very people he needs to speak into his life and challenge and encourage him.

Can you hear the anger and bitterness in his words? The unforgiveness has festered and blistered in his heart to the point that it is now affecting all of his relationships. He has cut out the very people he needs to speak into his life and challenge and encourage him.

In response, I wrote to the man and encouraged him to get into professional counseling as well as one-on-one marriage counseling. I reminded him that if the unforgiveness and anger were left unresolved, they would undoubtedly wreck his marriage and his entire life.

Another person wrote the following:

I agree with the fact that we must forgive to be forgiven, but my question is how do you forget? In my personal case,

I forgave a long time ago, but I have come to a place where I really don't care in the least for this person. I really don't care what happens in that person's life or that of her family. I just can't shake this feeling of not caring. I don't know if it is because I really have not forgiven. Please let me know. If I want really bad things to happen to this other person, have I forgiven her? This person talks a lot about others, is unsupportive to people and will stab you in the back to protect her own image. People leave our organization all the time because of this person. It is to the point that I don't want to be anywhere near her or be involved with her. I have prayed for answers but have found none. So I ask, Have I truly forgiven?

The answer is no. True forgiveness means forgiving in your heart even your worst enemy, which pushes the release button for what has been done to you. In this next section, let me answer this issue more completely. We'll look at the four keys to forgiving a difficult spouse.

Keys to Forgiving a Difficult Spouse

Key 1: Fight Your Attitude of Retaliation

From an early age, we learn about retaliation. If someone hits you, hit back. If someone says something mean, say something mean in response. If someone makes you feel bad, make him feel worse. Along the way, we bought into the lie that if we can make someone else hurt worse than we do, then maybe we won't hurt so bad.

You and your spouse know each other like few other people. You know each other's strengths and gifts, but you also know your weaknesses and soft spots. You know the areas where your spouse is particularly tender or susceptible to being hurt. You know how to get to your spouse, and he or she knows how to get to you. In a marriage relationship, retaliation cuts the deepest.

In His great love, Jesus forbids retaliation.
Though it may feel good for a split second,
God knows that the damage to you and to
the other person can last a lifetime.

In His great love, Jesus forbids retaliation. Though it may feel good for a split second, God knows that the damage to you and to the other person can last a lifetime. God knows that whatever pain we may try to dole out, the pain we're left with will be far greater.

Resisting the urge to retaliate is not easy, but Jesus never said it would be easy or come naturally. Sometimes biting your lip or turning the other cheek is one of the hardest things you'll ever have to do; but the good news is that you don't have to do it on your own. As you rest in the power of Christ as the Vine, waiting for the "sap" of His Spirit to flow His power and love and forgiveness into you, you will find yourself wanting to care for the person who hurt you. Although the human compulsion to retaliate seems normal, it is a product of sin. We must confess our weakness and wait for God's grace to empower us to love the offending person just as Jesus does.

I continually picture my life "stuck" within the Vine and wait for evidence that His love has reached my heart and produced "fruit." The fruit of the Spirit is love, joy, peace and all the other characteristics of Christ. I can't manufacture those qualities; I must wait for them to come out of me as I keep myself humble in the knowledge that I am truly "poor in Spirit." I cannot, under any human method, make myself love as Christ does. But He gives love freely to the humble. That's my job: to remain humble and dependent on Him.

As God's love begins to saturate your soul, you won't go after your spouse's weak spots. Instead of making your spouse or the offense your object of anger, you choose to take personal responsibility for what you are feeling and for your response. If you have already received the power to stop trying to change your mate and work only on yourself, then do it; but if not, wait for His love to flow through your branch of the Vine and form the love-fruit your spouse can enjoy.

One woman who had left her husband said, "I just can't stand the thought of going back into that situation. He offended me in so many ways, and he never comforted me when I needed it. I just can't go back."

I asked her if she'd be willing to teach her husband how to comfort her. She gave me a funny look and asked, "What do you mean by teach him?"

"When you are in a stressful situation or when you're discouraged, how do you want him to treat you?" I asked.

"I'd like him to put both arms around me and gently hold me," she explained. "Then I'd want him to tell me that he understood or at least that he was trying to understand."

"Well, why don't you teach him that?" I pressed.

"You're kidding! He'd think I was crazy. And besides, why should I have to teach him? He should do it on his own. I'd feel stupid having to tell him things like that."

I changed my approach a little. "Has he ever said things to you like, 'Honey, I don't know what you want me to do when you're discouraged. Should I cry, or kiss you or what?'"

Her eyes lit up and she said, "Yeah, it's amazing the number of times he's said that he didn't know what to do or how to act or what to say. I even remember him saying, 'You just tell me what you want me to do.' But I always thought he was being sarcastic, and I was offended because he couldn't figure it out by himself. I thought that if I had to tell him, it really wouldn't mean anything. Do you mean that some men really need to be taught the little things, like how to hold a woman tenderly?"

My answer was a firm "Yes!"

A lot of men avoid soft words and tender comfort because they have never been taught how to use them. Also, they simply don't understand the positive effects that these actions can have on their wives or the sense of wellbeing they themselves will receive. I have found that once a man has learned why and how to comfort, he gains a real appreciation for the role it plays in his marital relationship.

Key 2: Recognize that You Can Only Change Yourself

Though everything inside of you may scream otherwise, you are not responsible for changing the behavior of your spouse.

Many people have given up hope that their marriage will ever be better. When a woman's hope for a better marriage has faded, her attractiveness to her husband diminishes and the life of the relationship gradually declines. Regardless of how discouraged you may feel, however, it is never too late to rekindle your hope and bring renewed life into your relationship with your spouse.

---

*When a woman's hope for a better marriage
has faded, her attractiveness to her
husband diminishes and the life of the
relationship gradually declines.*

Shortly after their wedding, Denise was shocked at the difference between Jerry's behavior as a boyfriend and as a husband. For the first few months, she encountered increased pressure and resistance from him. One day when she was sick, she tried to share her feelings of weakness with him, telling him how much she needed his comfort and help around the house. Jerry's offhand reply was, "Oh, come on, get up, you can do it." He went on to imply that his mother never acted that way when she was sick.

Denise became discouraged; but after joining a group of couples with whom I meet, she made a commitment to pursue a better marriage.

Jerry didn't change overnight; in fact, things got worse before they got better. He continued with his inconsiderate behavior on several other occasions. But the story didn't end with Jerry's sarcasm. Because Denise had made a commitment to endure the pressure that sometimes comes from a husband when a wife begins to pursue a better marriage, Jerry has changed. But for several months, he watched Denise working on only herself. She actually learned how to thank God during difficult times with Jerry, because trials are one method God uses to "prune" us for greater growth. He uses the pain we feel during a trial to give us empathy, gracefulness, gentleness, love and a host of other godly qualities. That's why Paul could tell us to give thanks in all circumstances, for this is the will of God in Christ Jesus (see 1 Thess. 5:18).

Now Jerry has entered into the same commitment to build a better marriage. He is becoming more and more sensitive to Denise and now takes an active part in assuming many of the household responsibilities. That alone has helped draw them much closer, but Jerry is also beginning to respect Denise, her unique qualities and her unique sensitivities.

You may or may not encounter pressure or resistance as you begin a more active pursuit of a better marriage, but it's important that you commit yourself to endure any pressure that may come. If you wait for your spouse to initiate a better relationship, it may be a long, long wait.

When Jesus taught, He often used hyperbole, which means that He took a teaching to an extreme to emphasize a point. In Luke 6:29-31, Jesus says, "If someone strikes you on one cheek, turn to him the other also. If someone takes your cloak, do not stop him from taking your tunic. Give to everyone who asks you, and if anyone takes what belongs to you, do not demand it back. Do to others as you would have them do to you." Notice that throughout this passage, Jesus is not focusing on what is done to you. His focus is on your response. Jesus says that even if someone is taking something from you that isn't rightfully theirs, you are still accountable for your response to God.

Do not retaliate. Don't try to hurt the person who hurts you. Embrace the power of God's love by not trying to rob the person who steals from you. Treat him better than you have been treated, and then the glory goes to the Lord.

Puny human love doesn't go very far, does it? We look forward to seeing a multitude of Christ-followers demonstrating the very nature of Christ because they are rooted and grounded in His love.

Key 3: Love Your Spouse Unconditionally

We have some great local television commercials for a bank in which the commentator says, "We're your community bank. We love you. We are here to serve you. We have cookies and coffee in our lobby." It's such a great sentiment, but I can't help but think about what happens when one of their clients misses a series of mortgage payments. Does the loan officer from the bank deliver cookies and coffee with a smile to the person's home? Probably not. The loan officer is not going to say, "Oh, we see you didn't make a house payment in five months. That's no problem, you just keep the house!"

While cookies and coffee are a nice perk, they are based on a contract that you will do things a certain way. You will pay your loans back on time. You will play by their rules.

Instead of harboring bitterness or unresolved anger toward your spouse, you don't wait for him (or her) to do something that warrants your offer of forgiveness.

Jesus teaches something completely different: As His followers, we must not place conditions or establish an unwritten contract in order to love someone. We are to love unconditionally, just as God loves us. That means that instead of harboring bitterness or unresolved anger toward your spouse, you don't wait for him (or her) to do something that warrants your offer of forgiveness. You can't place conditions on forgiveness.

What did Jesus say when He hung on the cross? Did He wait for the onlookers to repent? No. Instead, Jesus asked His Father to forgive them because they didn't know what they were doing. Can you have the attitude of Christ toward every person you meet, no matter how deep the offense? Yes, you can! You can when you choose to love unconditionally under the influence of God's Spirit.

Key 4: Respond to God Instead of Reacting to Your Spouse
Tommy Nelson, pastor of Denton Bible Church, says that if you habitually harbor unforgiveness in your heart, you need

to call your faith into question. That may seem harsh, but your ability to love and forgive is based on the love and forgiveness you have received from God. If you can't forgive people of their offenses, then you have to ask yourself the tough question: *Where am I in my relationship with the Lord?*

I once heard Chuck Swindoll remark, "Man is never more like a beast than when he kills. He is most like man when he is unforgiving and he is most like God when he is forgiving." We will become forgiving people if we, the branches, abide in Christ, who is the Vine, and wait for His power to help us live as He wants us to live.

The Bible says that the way we love each other tells the world that we are followers of Jesus, that we are disciples of Jesus Christ (see John 13:35). How are you responding to God? Can you put aside the person and the offense that you formerly held in an attitude of unforgiveness and respond that you are ready to move forward with Him? Your faith will only go as far as you are willing to let God infuse you with His love.

In the parable of the unmerciful servant, Jesus teaches that the more you understand the forgiveness God has given you, the easier it will be for you to forgive others (see Matt. 18:21-35). God has forgiven us a great debt, a debt for which we deserved death. That is what our sin brought upon us; the Bible says, "The wages of sin is death, but the gift of God is eternal life in Jesus Christ our Lord" (Rom. 6:23). If He has forgiven you for all of your offenses toward Him and others, what offense has been brought upon you that you cannot forgive?

Release Your Spouse to God

Early in our marriage, Norma came to the unpleasant realization that I was also married to my work. The long hours I spent at the office frequently included evenings and weekends. This pattern left Norma alone a great deal of the time in the trenches with our energetic little girl and boys.

When I was home, my mind was filled with all things work, which also left little time for our marriage. Understandably, Norma felt neglected and would try to tell me. She'd point out that I wasn't there for her needs or to help with the parenting. But to me, her efforts to communicate her feelings sounded more like nagging, so I ignored it—as many men do!

Imagine my surprise when one day I came home and sensed a calm spirit in our home. Norma's face was peaceful, not tense as it usually was. Instead of the customary harsh words, her conversation was quiet, and she was more interested in asking me how my day had gone than in relating her hectic activities.

A few days later, with peace still in our house, I asked what had happened.

I realized I wasn't trusting God
with our marriage and family,
and so I decided to stop complaining
and start praying.

"I got tired of fighting you," she explained calmly. "I realized I wasn't trusting God with our marriage and family, and so I decided to stop complaining and start praying. I've told God that I'd like you to spend more time at home and help with the kids. Since God knows my needs, I know He'll make the necessary changes."

I was instantly convicted. Her quiet words forced me to look inside myself and see that my priorities were wrong. And that wasn't all. Because Norma had changed, I *wanted* to spend more time at home. Besides, if she had prayed that God would change me, I wasn't sure what He might do to "encourage" me to change!

Norma realized she couldn't change things on her own. She needed help from God. Rather than complain, she started to pray. I was fascinated by her immediate change in attitude, so I asked her what exactly she had prayed.

She told me, "I prayed, *Lord, thank You that all I need is You. You know I want a good relationship with Gary, and that I want him to spend more time at home. You also understand that I'm not strong physically. I'm so tired, and I don't feel I can last much longer under this strain. I'm coming to You with these requests because I know that if I need Gary at home, You can make it happen. Or You can take away my desire for him to be home. I'm going to stop fighting Gary and instead ask You either to change him or to meet my needs in some other way."*

Norma stopped expecting life from me and started expecting it from God. She realized that I not only *would* not, but *could* not energize her, so she went to the Source of life.

Some may think Norma just disguised her selfishness by asking God to change me instead of nagging me to change.

I disagree. Some may also think I was in the wrong—that I was the one who needed to change. To that, I agree. But Norma wasn't the one, as admirable as her desires were, who could induce a change in me. Only God could handle that task.

I encourage wives to ask God for a good relationship with their husbands and children. And vice versa. That request isn't selfish. A good relationship benefits not only the praying spouse, but also the entire family's health; and that health can spread to the Christian community and ultimately throughout our nation and the world. It also glorifies God, because a godly marriage is a picture of our relationship with Jesus Christ.

When we're in the habit of seeking fulfillment from the world, we won't learn to look to God as the Source of life. It took Norma and me several years before looking to the Lord became our natural first response. Occasionally, we still catch ourselves focusing on someone or something other than God.

When we really seek to connect with God individually, we unleash a powerful force in our life and our marriage. Norma told me how glad she was that she stopped nagging me and started praying to God for change. "I have more energy," she said, "and I enjoy the time we spend together. That would never have happened had I kept trying to change the situation myself. In fact, nagging wore me out."

Hope for a Spiritually Mixed Marriage

Every Sunday, I (Ted) meet families in which the wife or husband brings the kids to church while the spouse stays at home. The reason? The person's mate has no interest in following Christ or growing in faith. It is difficult for a believer to be married to a nonbeliever. It is even more difficult to be married to someone who professes faith in Jesus yet lives like a pagan.

If you find yourself in a spiritually difficult marriage, there is still hope for your spouse to change and for you to have a great marriage. But the solution will go against your grain. It may be the opposite of what you want to do. It will feel at times as if you are losing, but hold on.

Try a new approach, like Norma did. Consider 1 Peter 3:1-4:

> Wives, in the same way be submissive to your husbands so that, if any of them do not believe the word, they may be won over without words by the behavior of their wives, when they see the purity and reverence of your lives. Your beauty should not come from outward adornment, such as braided hair and the wearing of gold jewelry and fine clothes. Instead, it should be that of your inner self, the unfading beauty of a gentle and quiet spirit, which is of great worth in God's sight.

This passage is the whole reason I have modified the use of the unity candle in wedding ceremonies. In the past, the two moms would walk the aisle and light two candles: one for the bride and one for the groom. Then at some point in the ceremony, the bride and groom would take their individual candles and light a larger center candle, which represents oneness or blending the two together. Up to that point, I'm still good. But I've changed the part when the couple traditionally would blow out their individual candles. I now ask them to leave both of those candles lit. Why?

Because while a couple may start out following Jesus together, there may come a day when one spouse gives up faith and stops growing. Does that mean that the one who wants to still pursue Christ is stuck? Absolutely not!

There are three journeys at work here:

1. *Your spiritual journey.* You are 100-percent responsible to discover your gifts and be a good steward of your walk with Christ. Your mate is 0-percent responsible for this journey.

2. *Your mate's spiritual journey.* You are 0-percent responsible for this journey, but your mate is 100-percent responsible to discover his or her gifts and be a good steward of his or her walk with Christ.

3. *Your marital journey.* You both are to honor, encourage and assist each other throughout a lifetime of commitment.

If your spiritual journey is sustained by your spouse, what happens to you when he or she chooses to stop growing? That is why I am so encouraged when I see a single mom or dad bring their kids to church: They know their walk with Christ must continue.

But how do we do that with a forgiving spirit? There are plenty of times when I ask the spiritually single parent about their mate, and their bitterness starts to show. I tell them to take encouragement from 1 Peter 3. The passage says their spouse "may be won over without words." The temptation to change your mate brings about some extreme measures, but fight the urge to blast Christian radio around the house. Fight the urge to leave the Bible open on his or her nightstand or pillow. Fight the urge to read aloud during your devotions. Above all else, fight the urge to preach. Let your mate see you growing in the Lord.

What does growth in the Lord look like? It is characterized by unconditional love, joy, peace, patience, gentleness, kindness and self-control. The Bible calls this "the unfading beauty of a gentle and quiet spirit, which is of great worth in God's sight" (v. 4).

I (Gary) saw this same dynamic unfold in my marriage over the past six years. I now believe that I am 100-percent responsible for my own growth with God. I focus on that relationship partly by memorizing and meditating daily on a few key Bible passages that have so enriched me over these past few years.

Norma has watched me work on myself instead of trying to work on her, and she is now pursuing her own walk with God with so much more enthusiasm than when I was her "Holy Spirit," trying to manipulate a few changes I thought she needed in her life. What a mistake that was!

Six years ago, I gave up all attempts to "work" on her in any way, and today we are closer and so much more in love than at any other time in our 43 years of marriage.

In the next chapter, we will explore how to heal from sexual addiction and an affair. If these have not touched your own marriage, you probably know someone who has dealt with these devastations. We will highlight six requirements that make all the difference when it comes to breaking sexual addiction, and then we will look at how to heal from the devastating effects of an affair.

From GarySmalley.com

Q: *If someone says they have forgiven me, what do I do if they keep holding it over my head?*

A: Forgiveness is not just a one-time event; it is a process. Too many Christians get this point confused. We often hear, "If she forgave me, then she would be over this by now!"

That mindset is not realistic. If you have done something extremely hurtful and need to seek forgiveness, then you can't expect the healing to happen immediately. Your loved one will not get over the hurt right away; it takes time. Just because you have earnestly sought forgiveness and forgiveness has been given does not mean there will not be consequences for your actions.

In fact, depending on the severity of the hurt, the relationship may never fully recover from the pain. This isn't to say that we will suffer day after day, but it does mean that the pain may show up periodically even after the passage of years, sparked by some event that triggers the memory. The pain isn't as severe as when it first happened, but it still hurts.

I think back periodically on my first several years of marriage and am sickened by some of the things I said to Norma. I don't ruminate over them, but sometimes they just pop up in my memory. When that happens, I'm reminded what a jerk I was at different points in our first year of marriage.

I think occasional remembrance of these types of things is one way God helps us stay humble. It's hard to be overly confident about our emotional or spiritual maturity when we remember how things used to be. We can be encouraged, however, that our pain only gives us the opportunity to be better Christians. Walking through those valleys, we feel a bonding with God that the good times just can't produce. Lessons learned about His loyal love are what inspired David to write, "The Lord is my shepherd, I shall not want . . . *though I walk through the valley of the shadow of death,* I will fear no evil; for thou art with me" (Ps. 23:1,4, *KJV,* emphasis added). Talk about bonding! David was a man whose heart cleaved to God's because he had faced the fires and God saw him through.

In the same way, when difficult times face each of us, we can respond in thankfulness to God, confident that the experience will make us more trusting of Him. You may not be growing from the trial today, but my experience has shown that years from now, your perspective on the situation will change. If you choose to grow from it, you will change for the better.

Renew

Recovering from an Affair or Sexual Addiction

I (Ted) was caught off guard by the phone call. It was late at night and the caller ID listed an out-of-state number. I summoned my best "of course I'm awake" voice and picked up the phone. I immediately recognized the familiar voice of my long-time friend Matt. "Hey, Matt," I said with as much energy as I could muster. "Long time no hear. What's going on?"

"I need to talk," Matt said.

"Yeah, man, what's up?"

"I've made a terrible mistake!" he said.

From his tone of voice, I knew that something was seriously wrong. "Matt, did you have an affair?" I asked without hesitation.

"I wish," Matt said. Then he began rambling. Though his words were forced, they were also nonsensical. I pressed him again: "What happened, Matt?"

That's when he confessed, "I have been involved in a secret sin that I have been able to hide my entire life. But this week I was found out. The authorities showed up at my house and confiscated my computer. I am being accused of activities that are too embarrassing to mention. I have lost my family. My life is over."

In the upcoming pages, we'll explore what happened to Matt and his family, but this chapter isn't about Matt's addiction. The real story is about his recovery: It's an unforgettable testimony to God's redemption and healing. We'll also look at six requirements for breaking the addiction. And we'll look at how spouses can heal after an affair.

Breaking the Addiction

Shortly after that late-night phone call, Matt and I met for breakfast. At the time, he was not ready to expose his sin to me.

"Matt, whatever you say to me right now will not leave this table," I assured him. "And I will not look at you as a pervert or as someone who is beyond hope."

Yet throughout our meal, Matt's words were guarded. Even his posture displayed a closed spirit. He was withdrawn into a self-created prison. He could not find a way to forgive himself.

For a long while, I had no idea the extent of Matt's addiction. It wasn't until a year later that I received this handwritten letter from him:

Hi Ted. I hope this letter finds you and your family doing well. I want to first apologize for not typing this out on a computer. I recently decided to not use the computer for an undetermined amount of time. I want all temptation gone from my life.

I want to thank you for your kindness you showed me during my deepest struggles. Your reached out to me and did not judge me. Which brings me to the second reason I am writing you.

When we went to breakfast that morning, you told me something I could not believe or even comprehend at that time. You told me that no matter what I had done, you would not reject me or turn away from me. Well, I could not accept or believe that. After all, my entire life I was surrounded by just the opposite of that. While there with you, all I wanted to do was die. I would tell myself to live but my body could only shake. My mind was discouraged and filled with shame and guilt.

Ted, I have always felt bad because I was unwilling to trust what you said to me to be true. I was not honest with you or myself, which is something I have really had to work on: BEING HONEST.

The truth is I fell harder than anyone knows. My fears of rejection over the taboo lines I crossed scare me. My new pastor, who is also my dear friend, has still accepted me despite the homosexual encounters, but I am not sure others will, and I doubt my family will.

Thanks for your hope in me,

Matt

The road to healing and forgiveness for Matt has been a long one, but here are six requirements that were crucial to his restoration.

Requirement 1: Hide Nothing

For Matt, the real healing and restoration began when he realized that nothing can be hidden from God. While he could hide his behavior from his family, he couldn't hide from God.

Psalm 139 is a reminder of the fact that God is all-knowing (omniscient) and everywhere present (omnipresent):

> O LORD, you have searched me and you know me. You know when I sit and when I rise; you perceive my thoughts from afar. You discern my going out and my lying down; you are familiar with all my ways. Before a word is on my tongue you know it completely, O LORD (vv. 1-4).

Matt realized that when he confessed his sins to God, God was not surprised by any of them. He knew them all. He saw them when they were happening—in real time.

For anyone who has ever struggled with an affair or with sexual addiction, coming clean is the first step to renewing his or her relationship with Christ and others. God has given us the wonderful gift of fellowship to walk with other believers to help us be healed from our sin. James 5:16 says, "Therefore confess your sins to each other and pray for each other so that you may be healed. The prayer of a righteous man is powerful and effective." For Matt, the first step was the hardest. Denial, anxiety, disbelief and shame marked his emotions. But until those emotions came out in the form of words, Matt was stuck. He had to express his sin and emotions before he could move on to the next requirement.

Requirement 2: Receive Forgiveness

Once Matt asked God for forgiveness, he had to receive that forgiveness. The guilt and shame of what he had done weighed on his soul. Not only did he feel remorse, but he felt self-hatred. He wanted to hide from his family and God, but he realized that it's not enough to ask for forgiveness; you have to receive it. You have to let go of the guilt and shame and see yourself as God now sees you.

Psalm 103:8-13 describes just how far God goes to erase sin when we ask for forgiveness:

> The LORD is compassionate and gracious, slow to anger, abounding in love. He will not always accuse, nor will he harbor his anger forever; he does not treat us as our sins deserve or repay us according to our iniquities. For as high as the heavens are above the earth, so great is his love for those who fear him; as far as the east is from the west, so far has he removed our transgressions from us. As a father has compassion on his children, so the LORD has compassion on those who fear him.

Matt had to begin reprogramming his mind in light of God's forgiveness, mercy and grace. He began to soak his mind and soul in God's Word, and cultivated the viewpoint of Psalm 139:17-18: "How precious to me are your thoughts, O God! How vast is the sum of them! Were I to count them, they would outnumber the grains of sand. When I awake, I am still with you." By meditating on God's Word, Matt found that God's thoughts began to replace his own thoughts.

Requirement 3: Redefine Yourself

Once Matt asked for forgiveness and received forgiveness, he had to redefine himself. Matt was no longer someone who kept secrets from his family. He was no longer a sex addict. He was no longer a consumer of porn. Instead, he was now God's child: forgiven, redeemed and in the process of being made whole. The way Matt saw himself was crucial to his recovery.

Pastor Rick Warren from Saddleback Church originally opened my eyes to this truth. While the program Celebrate Recovery in which Matt participated parallels many of the teachings from Alcoholics Anonymous, there are some teachings that are very different. He told me, "Instead of standing up and identifying ourselves by our weakness ('Hi, I'm John, and I am an alcoholic'), we identify ourselves by our strength in God."

A person must find expressions every day that remind him (her) of his (her) worth in Christ. "I am loved by God" is a great start.

"I am a son, or daughter, of the Most High."

"Hi, I'm Matt, and God knew me before I was even in my mother's womb."

"Hi, I'm Matt, and God is crazy about me. His love toward me has never wavered. He cannot see my sin because Jesus stands in the way."

This requirement is based on 2 Corinthians 5:17: "Therefore, if anyone is in Christ, he is a new creation; the old has gone, the new has come!"

As Matt began to redefine who he was in light of God's strength, love, power and redemption, the transformation was unmistakable. As of the writing of this book, Matt has celebrated one year of sobriety from sexual addiction, and I couldn't be more proud of him. Through God's grace, proper accountability and his own awareness, I know that Matt will only continue to grow stronger and find deeper levels of healing in his heart, his mind and his marriage.

Requirement 4: Recruit Assistants

We all need people in our life who will do two things: encourage and rebuke. I would be lost without these in my life, and Gary has a knack for doing both on a regular basis. What makes Gary so great is that he is balanced between the two: He encourages *and* rebukes. Being out of balance sets a person up for failure. If you have a friend who only encourages and never rebukes, then you will live a puffed up, exaggerated life. On the other hand, if you have a friend who only rebukes and never encourages, then you will live a deflated, discouraged life. Neither one is healthy.

Matt needed, and still needs, accountability assistants in his life. These assistants must be recruited; Matt needed to be the one to invite the assistant in for accountability. Self-proclaimed accountability partners don't work. Matt needed to feel safe in order to stay open about his struggles.

I am honored to serve as one of Matt's assistants. When I am asked to hold someone accountable in the area of sexual addiction or temptation, one of the first things I do is encourage them to purchase an accountability software. "Covenant Eyes" just so happens to be my software of choice. When it is installed, the accountability assistant has access to the computer of his or her recovering friend. Each week, I get a detailed (and I mean *detailed!*) report of almost every keystroke Matt or others make on his computer. (Just recently, I was invited to become an assistant for a buddy across the country. He is a young unmarried man who has struggled with his addiction to pornography since junior high. Shortly after I began receiving reports on my friend's computer, I noticed the activity online going downhill. He emailed to say that it was because he was sharing a computer with a roommate. I called to have a little chat. I told him that it rendered the accountability report useless if he was sharing a computer with someone who was looking at porn. He agreed. I guess you could consider that a gentle rebuke. He quickly denied computer access to his roommate.)

If you struggle with sexual temptation, recruit an assistant. You don't need 20 people holding you accountable, but you definitely need a few that will offer you a healthy balance between rebuke and encouragement.

Requirement 5: Practice Spiritual Disciplines
Recently, one of the largest U.S. churches in Chicago released a study of their congregation that charted their spiritual growth over the last 25 years. They discovered that people who are growing in Christ practice three spiritual disciplines:

1. Consistent prayer time
2. Regular quiet time
3. Great relationships

Once you starve your soul of the toxins you have allowed in your body, such as pornography, you must replace them with a new diet. Instead of heading to the computer at 3:00 A.M. when you can't sleep, head to an easy chair and turn on a lamp to read your Bible. (If you don't have a cozy corner set up to read, as soon as possible go to a furniture store and pick out a comfy chair, a new end table and a lamp.) Make this your prayer closet or personal study. Open your Bible. Pray. Invest in your environment so that you have a place to go and enjoy spending time with the Lord.

Requirement 6: Write Letters and Read Books

Matt no longer uses a computer. He doesn't even have one in his home that could be fired up late at night in a moment of weakness. The letters I receive from Matt seem strange in this era of email: They are handwritten, neatly folded in an envelope with a stamp on the outside and they get delivered to my home and placed in the mailbox. I've commented several times to Amy that I think I'm going to buy Matt a quill this Christmas!

Matt also reads a lot more books these days. I think he is on to something. We live in a sex-saturated culture—it is everywhere you turn. Movies, commercials, reality television and sitcoms can contain sexually explicit material that is a hindrance to the holiness to which we are called to live. Matt now draws a strong line and stands clear behind it.

Recovering from Your Spouse's Addiction or Affair

While the road to recovery has been difficult for Matt, some would argue that it's been even more difficult for Matt's wife, Teresa. The shame, embarrassment and betrayal that Teresa felt were overwhelming and pushed her almost to the breaking point. But there, she discovered God, grace and growth like she had never experienced before.

Earlier on the night when Matt called me, Teresa reacted to the authorities entering her home with shock, uncertainty and embarrassment. She had more questions than answers. (Actually, she had *all* questions and *no* answers.)

Teresa knew that the investigators were not there for her; the only reasons she used the computer were to email her mom or pay her bills online. When she asked her husband what had happened, Matt had no words. He had nothing to say. He could have denied everything and fought it, but he was caught, and he knew it.

She felt duped and betrayed. Teresa's road to recovery and healing was much different from Matt's, but just as difficult— if not more so. How did she begin to heal? Here are several things she did to find healing for herself and her marriage.

Take Time to Mourn

We have taught throughout this book how to turn your trials into treasures. We have looked at rejoicing in your pain because pain produces endurance; endurance builds character; and character builds hope. This process is real, but it is not immediate. Teresa did not start jumping up and down for joy in the kitchen, praising God for an opportunity to grow. Instead, she needed to take time to grieve the death of intimacy in her marriage.

Too often, women and men skip this first step. They try to jump to the solution or to the recovery phase of healing without taking time to acknowledge that something devastating has happened. A part of the marriage has died, and it can only come to life again if we acknowledge the loss.

Wisely, Teresa took time to acknowledge the pain she was feeling. She surrounded herself with friends and Christian counselors who affirmed that her feelings of hurt, frustration and anger were healthy.

Remember the quiz from chapter 2? We invited you to ask yourself two key questions about your anger:

Question 1:
What am I angry about?

Question 2:
What am I going to do with my anger?

When Teresa asked the first question, she recognized that her anger was about broken promises and vows, and about adultery and loss of trust. She needed time to understand and process her anger, but she also knew she had to have an outlet for it that was not destructive. That's why she began to create boundaries.

Create Boundaries

I have counseled many couples who have been ripped apart by sexual addiction. Matt and Teresa's situation is far from unique, but in every case there need to be some healthy boundaries created.

You begin to create boundaries by guarding your heart and body from any level of perversion. It is okay to deny sex to a spouse who is sexually addicted. Why? Mainly because sexual addicts are, typically, great manipulators and deceivers. They have learned the craft of hiding their addiction from those around them. They wait until the family goes to bed to go online. They position the office furniture to enable them to minimize the window when someone enters the room. Many addicts downplay the extent of their addiction.

You must stop exposing yourself to potentially life-threatening diseases, and you must discover the full extent of the addiction. You can only do this by creating a healthy boundary.

Become a Learner

Part of recovering from your mate's addiction, and starting down the road of forgiveness, comes by understanding a bit more about sexual addiction. For Teresa, it meant no longer seeing Matt as a pervert, but as a child of God who made a horrendous mistake. She now recognizes how sin took over and dominated his life. She sees the timeline of his fall and can see the unguarded moments in their marriage.

Most sexual addicts start young. From the first exposure to the getting caught, it is important to understand the deadly cycle. Dr. Mark Laaser is one of the nation's fore-most experts on sexual addiction. He has educated men and women all over the world on the characteristics of sexual addiction. This list will help as you gain understanding into the mind of your mate:

Characteristics of Sexual Addiction

1. The first step in Alcoholics Anonymous is to admit that you are powerless. Sexual addiction is unmanageable. It takes you further than you want to go and keeps you for longer than you want to stay. The heart of an addict says, "I don't trust that God can meet all my needs." It is the struggle that Paul speaks of in Romans 7:15: "I do not understand what I do. For what I want to do I do not do, but what I hate I do."

2. Research into neurochemical tolerance teaches us that the brain adjusts to whatever chemical you dose it with. It is for this reason that one beer does not make an alcoholic drunk. Addiction is fed by creating tolerance. As the addict is stimulated sexually, adrenaline produces dopamine. The more dopamine is in the brain and the longer the periods of time it is produced, the more we want. The brain adjusts and then needs more of these chemicals to feel the same level of pleasure. That is

why Paul says in Romans 12:1-2 that we are to "be transformed by the renewing of your mind." Much like Matt's progression, sexual addiction gets away from the one it possesses. (By the way, this is what the peddlers of Internet pornography are counting on. It is part of their marketing plan.)

3. Sexual addiction is used to escape feelings. It is a coping mechanism for feelings such as sadness, loneliness, depression and anxiety.

4. There is a level of entitlement in many sexual addicts. They think, *I deserve to have my needs met.*

This last characteristic makes so much sense but was a major eye-opener for me (Ted). I reward myself with food, and I have to guard myself against a food addiction. In the marriage seminars that I do around the country with Gary, I am usually the last speaker on Friday evening, with the session ending around 10:00 P.M. After a little meet-and-greet time with folks, I generally leave the church or hall around 11:00 P.M., and I'm usually by myself when I head back to the hotel.

I can't tell you the number of times I have driven past a Waffle House or Krispy Kreme and said to myself, *I worked hard tonight. I gave it 110 percent! I deserve to eat whatever I want.* Thankfully, 99 times out of 100, I am too exhausted to stop; but I must fight the temptation nonetheless. If I have a stressful day at the church office in counseling or staff meetings, my temptation is to come home and grab some junk food. Why? Because I deserve it. That is a feeling of entitlement, and it is no different in the life of a sex addict. They act on their addiction while thinking things like:

- *My wife won't put out, so I deserve to have my needs met.*
- *I'm working long, hard hours and do not have time to be a 12-hour lover to my wife, or nurture intimacy. What's the harm in taking a few minutes to look at a website or two and relieve myself? I at least deserve that.*

This is also why pastors are so susceptible to sexual addiction. With all the "good" ministers do on a daily basis, we can get this attitude with God: *Look at all I am doing for people and You. Certainly there can't be any harm in indulging myself just a little. I deserve this.*

The characteristics that we've just provided do not do full justice to the subject of sexual addiction. For more information, read materials on the subject, interview recovering addicts, get counseling and do whatever else you must do to learn the source and cycle of this addiction. Studying sexual addiction will help you with the next step of recovery.[1]

Do Not Take the Blame

Recognize that you are not the reason for your mate's stumble, struggle or addiction. He or she is 100-percent responsible for his or her actions.

No doubt, Teresa has asked herself the question, *Where did I fail Matt?* While that question can help her see herself in the breakdown of the marriage, it does not diminish Matt's responsibility for his sin.

Scripture challenges the believing, committed spouse who lives with an unbelieving spouse to continue on his or her faith journey. A husband who sees his wife drifting in the marriage or in her walk with Christ has one responsibility: He must pursue the Lord with all of his heart, soul, mind and strength. Her drifting is not an excuse for his.

Choose to Forgive

That's right! Sexual addiction is forgivable! As a follower of Jesus, you are required to forgive. Even if your spouse is unrepentant, you must forgive. Forgiveness has nothing to do with whether or not they change, but it has everything to do with you and your relationship with God.

For Teresa, choosing to forgive has not been easy. But slowly she has found that it is getting easier. As much pain and hurt as her husband caused, she looks at the forgiveness God offers her and responds to His forgiveness with a heart that is willing to forgive her husband more and more each day.

If you are not yet to the point where you can take this step, then meditate on the Scripture passages found in the Meditations for Forgiveness section at the end of this book. Continue to cry out to God for His Holy Spirit to empower you to heed and obey His command to forgive.

If you, like Teresa, make it through all of these steps, then you are ready to move forward.

Assist Your Spouse's Recovery

Assisting your spouse on his or her road to recovery is both challenging and rewarding. I believe that the best thing you can do for your mate is to say, "I am going to become an assistant to you on this journey without taking responsibility. I am going to look to God." In other words, rather than trying to change your spouse or play moral police, pray for your spouse and challenge him or her to get the help and support he or she needs.

Genesis 2:25 says, "The man and his wife were both naked, and they felt no shame." What does that mean? Adam and Eve were together; they had oneness; they weren't afraid or embarrassed; they weren't criticized or blamed or rejected or disconnected. They were together—walls down, clothes off—and were not ashamed. But then what happened in Genesis 3? The Fall. They ate the forbidden fruit and sin entered our world.

What if Eve had eaten of the fruit, but Adam had not? Now, that's a scenario you don't hear explored in too many sermons, but we can infer that Eve would have died and Adam would have lived. Let's go a step further. Adam could have laid down his life for Eve. The grave could not have held him, because he was sinless. He could have paid the ultimate price, but he didn't. Instead he ate, and then blamed God and the woman when he said, "The woman you put here with me" is at fault (see Gen. 3:12).

Is this alternate scenario a stretch? Not at all! It happened, but not in the first Adam. It happened in the second Adam, who is Jesus Christ:

Therefore, just as sin entered the world through one man, and death through sin, and in this way death came to all men, because all sinned—For if the many died by the trespass of the one man, how much more did God's grace and the gift that came by the grace of the one man, Jesus Christ, overflow to the many! (Rom. 5:13,15).

Your marriage may be full of death right now, but it is not out of reach of the blood of Jesus. He can heal you. He can heal your husband or wife. He can heal your marriage. He can restore your family. Jesus died to make it happen!

Actions that Protect Your Marriage

The real tragedy of infidelity is that many marriages that are marred by an affair end in divorce. In the blink of an eye, the trust and security that are the foundation for a healthy marriage are destroyed, and it takes years of dedicated work to rebuild the trust and security ripped away by an affair. The reason is simple. Have you ever attempted to walk down a frozen sidewalk after an ice storm? Although it's possible, there is always anxiety that a horrible fall might be straight ahead. What many couples fail to realize is that an absence of trust and security in a marriage is like condemning a person to live on that ice-covered sidewalk. Your mate is never truly free to relax because he or she is continually fighting to keep his or her footing.

To protect your marriage, you need to make a daily decision to have an affair-proof relationship. This protection

Can I Leave My Sexually Addicted Spouse?

We do not believe that addiction to pornography is a legitimate biblical reason to divorce your mate. If your spouse has a sexual addiction, we do advise you to create space until a definite plan for recovery and healing is in place. But in the end, we always default to saving the marriage.

Yet we know that your mate may have already made the decision to end the marriage by continuing in his or her dangerous behavior. Your spouse should not be allowed to hold the marriage hostage. Here is a simple test to determine if your mate is serious about recovery.

1. *Is the behavior relentless?* Is there a charge-ahead, egotistical attitude about the addiction?

2. *Is the behavior persistent?* Is there an "I ain't stoppin'" attitude?

3. *Is he or she unrepentant?* Is there an "I'm doing nothing wrong" attitude?

builds trust and security, which in turn melt the ice so that there is no fear of falling. Security from marital fidelity is built when we do four important things.

1. Make a Commitment to Grow

First, it's extremely important for you to make a commitment to keep growing in your relationship with your mate. According to author and psychologist Dr. Gary Oliver, sexual temptation increases as the satisfaction in the relationship decreases. In other words, the lower a person's relational happiness, the greater the temptation to medicate through some kind of addictive behavior such as sex, alcohol, work, and so on. In order to find out what your relationship needs, ask your mate: "What is something I could do that would cause our relationship to grow?" Begin making a list of specific things and pick one of them to do on a weekly basis.

2. Be Aware of Your Choices

Rationalization is a damaging force working against marital fidelity. Today there is an epidemic of "It's okay as long as you don't get caught" and "It's not that bad, everyone's doing it." A major battle is won when we stop asking what's *wrong* with certain choices and instead ask what's *right* with them.

Every day I read a short poem above my computer, and it has become the key for affair-proofing my own marriage:

The choices we make every day,
Dictate the life we lead.
To thine own self be true!

Basically, this is similar to a message from Jesus that Luke recorded in his Gospel: "Whoever can be trusted with very little can also be trusted with much" (16:10). In other words, how we handle the small things dictates how we react to the bigger things. I now start each day by thinking about the choices I'll make and how they will dictate my life. For example, if I spend too much time talking to a female coworker, I need to be aware of how this can weaken my defenses or make me susceptible for an affair, whether it is emotional or physical.

The last part, "To thine own self be true," simply means that as Christians, we must learn what God desires for our lives and remain true to His wishes.

Being aware of our choices leads into the third way to affair-proof your marriage.

3. Draw a Line and Stay Far Away!

While doing a seminar in Hawaii, my family and I were caught in a major storm. At one point, 30-foot waves were crashing against the hotel. It felt like we were being shelled by artillery. Wanting to get close to the monstrous waves, my father and I snuck past a sign that read "Dangerous Beyond This Point!" Standing near the water's edge, a gigantic wave suddenly broke and knocked us down. As we laughed and high-fived each other, we were confronted by hotel security. They explained that the waves weren't the only danger; the real problem was the rocks that were jarred loose each time a wave struck the shore. We had difficulty believing it until we saw pebbles imbedded in the side of the hotel.

The reason the hotel placed danger signs away from the water's edge was to create a buffer zone. In other words, the hotel wanted to leave room for error. This way, if someone made a mistake and crossed the line, hopefully he or she wouldn't be killed.

If you want to affair-proof your marriage, it's important to draw a line and then stay a safe distance behind it. For each person, the safety line will be different. Some people will not be able to take business trips with or work late with a coworker of the opposite sex. Others may not be able to meet a certain person for lunch or to work out at the gym. Whatever the situation, determine where you need to draw the line. Everyone makes mistakes, and having room before you fall over the edge can be the difference between weathering a compromising situation and losing your marriage.

4. Become Accountable to Someone

The final piece in the puzzle of maintaining marital fidelity is accountability, which is simply being responsible to another person or persons to account for the commitments you've made. If you desire to affair-proof your marriage, ask a good friend, a pastor, a Bible study group or trusted coworker for accountability. The important ingredient is having someone to ask the difficult questions, such as, "Did you compromise your standards last week?" or "Have you been getting your emotional needs met from someone other than your mate?" Ideally, these questions force us to carefully and prayerfully consider our choices because we know that someone will be checking.

If your desire is to build a protective hedge around your marriage, or if you and your mate are recovering from the damaging effects of an affair or a sexual addiction, you can melt the ice-covered sidewalks of your relationship by making the four principles to protect your marriage a part of your life. Rebuilt trust and increased security are sure to follow.

Though Matt and Teresa are not yet together, I am proud of both of them and the progress they have made. We're still waiting for the happily-ever-after that we know is coming. We already see glimpses of it.

In the next chapter, we will highlight the dangers of unresolved anger for your marriage. Then we will talk about how to foster forgiveness and then maintain forgiveness in your marriage.

From GarySmalley.com

Q: I have been married for more than 15 years, and I love my spouse; but I still find myself struggling with lust issues. I thought they would go away by now, but I find them growing stronger and I'm worried that I'm going to wake up in an affair one day. What should I do?

A: First, memorize Hebrews 13:4, which says, "Give honor to marriage, and remain faithful to one another in marriage" (*NLT*). God draws a firm line against casual and illicit sex. Marriage is where sex is to take place, and lust is an invitation to cross the line into sexual impropriety. You need to run away from its every offer or enticement. That may mean turning your head to look in a different direction when you're tempted, or it may be even more radical; you may need to make a change in your life so that you aren't working with a coworker who is particularly attractive to you. Whatever change you need to make—in your habits, schedule or work—by all means, do it, and do it fast! Through God's strength, you can overcome the temptation. You can stand firm.

Second, try what I (Gary) am doing to solve the lust issue in my life. When I see someone who catches my eye, I think, *Good job, God.* Instead of letting the temptation turn to lust (remember, temptation is not sin), I start wondering if that pretty girl's dad loves her. (I have counseled with enough people in the last couple of years to see how this stuff works.) I wonder if she is dressing that way to get attention because she had a dad who never gave her attention. I wonder if she is showing herself to every man she sees because she doesn't feel very secure about herself. I wonder if her husband is nice to her. I wonder if her husband really loves her.

Let me tell you: When you get in that mode, and you start praying for that person, it is difficult to jump into lust.

Note

1. We hosted a nationwide sexual addiction program called Freedom Begins Here. You can check it out at www.freedombeginshere.org. We also highly recommend Dr. Mark R. Laaser's book *Healing the Wounds of Sexual Addiction* (Grand Rapids, MI: Zondervan, 2004).

Remain

Maintaining Forgiveness in a Marriage

I (Gary) spent the majority of my marriage clueless about the link between forgiveness and tenderness. The times when Norma needed tenderness, I offered suggestions, speeches and duct tape. (After all, duct tape can fix anything.)

The home I grew up in was anything but tender. My dad did not teach me tenderness or how to show it toward a wife. If you're like me, and tenderness was not modeled in your childhood home, you need to stand up and break that generational curse.

Forgiveness flows out of tenderness. The posture of tenderness packages your words, emotions and actions into gentle deliveries. In a position of tenderness and gentleness, it is hard to maintain an unforgiving spirit.

Tenderness is the key to maintaining forgiveness in your marriage. Will you be a model of tenderness and forgiveness in your home? Your kids are watching, and they will learn how to be a mate for their future spouse from you.

Anger Opens Us to Darkness

I have a close friend named Larry. As a child, his father didn't drink often, but when he did, he drank hard. He physically abused Larry and his family. One evening, Larry was trying to get away from his father's pounding fists and hid between the refrigerator and cupboard. When his father found him, he demanded that he come out. Larry refused. Without an escape, Larry was trapped as his father kicked him until he bled.

That was Larry's childhood. That was his life. You can only imagine the level of anger in his heart. Tremendous rage brooded beneath his cool demeanor, and at times the anger exploded from within. He would start beating on his classmates. The anger distracted him from his schoolwork, destroyed his friendships and made him an outcast. The anger was ruining his life.

Why do I tell you this story? Because that's exactly what anger does. It takes you hostage and refuses to let go. Anger is like a ticking time bomb in your soul: You know it's there; you just don't know when it's going to explode.

In my more than 40 years of ministering, I've come to the conclusion that the number-one killer of love in any relationship is unresolved anger. While it's okay to get angry, it's not okay to stay mad for any length of time. Ephesians 4:26 instructs us to be angry but don't stay angry. Don't let the sun go down on your anger. Why? Because when you allow anger to fester in your heart, you give the enemy a foothold in your life.

Throughout this book, we have explored the issue of anger—especially anger in marriage—and the importance of breaking its cycle by taking responsibility for it. We have also looked at the importance of embracing a spirit of forgiveness and have provided practical tools, such as tips for crafting the perfect apology. And we have uncovered some of the darker roadblocks to forgiveness that every married couple faces.

As you have read, you may have experienced or are on your way to experiencing personal revival. You may have taken a huge step by forgiving someone from your past and you are now walking in joy like never before. It is the same joy a prisoner feels when set free. You have set your heart free. You are now at peace with Christ.

But here is a strong caution: You must guard your heart from allowing the anger to slip back in. In this chapter, we want to remind you of the dangers of unresolved anger in your marriage, and then we want to give you three ways to foster forgiveness and talk about how you can maintain forgiveness in your marriage.

Damage in the Darkness

Just how dangerous is anger? Check out 1 John 2:9-11:

> Anyone who claims to be in the light but hates his brother is still in the darkness. Whoever loves his brother lives in the light, and there is nothing in him to make him stumble. But whoever hates his brother is in the darkness and walks around in the darkness; he does not know where he is going, because the darkness has blinded him.

Not only does anger quench the light of God in our life, but when we allow anger in by refusing to forgive, our vision grows dim. We can't see as clearly. Our ability to discern is weakened. The worst part is that anger makes us unaware of what is really happening. In other words, the darkness of anger is actually blinding. Before we realize what has happened, we begin releasing it in our relationships and unleashing it on the people we love.

If you want your kids to be on fire for God and excited about their relationships with Jesus, let them see His Spirit free you from anger. Most of us have had this happen: Before church one day, you come down on your kids in anger. Maybe they did something small, but your anger was out of proportion. Now they're angry too. Sitting in church, both you and the kids (and probably your spouse) are sitting in darkness. Neither you nor your children are going to get much out of the sermon or be able to worship. The kids may even be tempted to act out and create a disruption. That's why the Bible instructs parents not to provoke their children to anger. Why? Because it places entire families in darkness and short-circuits all that God wants to do through you.

When I am angry, I can actually sense the darkness and blindness. Anger causes me to be less interested in spiritual things, such as praying—whether praying alone or with other people. Spiritual disciplines such as reading the Bible or memorizing Scripture seem pointless. My efforts to study the Scriptures go unrewarded. When I'm angry, reading the Bible is like eating sand: tasteless and uninteresting. My desire for God wanes day after day after day. I only recently realized that my continual anger was the source of my spiritual disinterest.

What specific damage does anger do?

Anger Makes Us Less Sensitive

It's harder for us to get intimate or close to people when we're angry. Angry people have a difficult time becoming close friends. Here's the reason: Angry people sabotage relationships because they don't feel comfortable being close. They say and do things to keep other people at a distance.

Imagine that you're trying to love your spouse or your kids and they block you out. They don't let you touch them; or when you say, "I love you," they don't say anything back to you. You probably wonder, *What's going on here?*

Almost always it's because they have anger tucked away in their hearts, and it's growing inside, breeding dissension and rebellion. When there is love and peace in a home, most kids automatically and naturally accept their parents' values. But if anger is present, kids find the things that they don't like about their parents and hone in on those things.

Anger also makes you less sensitive in your marriage. When anger is allowed to get a foothold, you find yourself less sensitive to your spouse, less willing to serve and less quick to forgive. That's why maintaining forgiveness in a marriage is so crucial to the health of the relationship.

Anger Consumes Intimacy

Anger is like an ember that never goes out. It may look like it's dormant, but when the wind of right circumstances comes along, it flames up. Knowing there's something there—an ember of anger—but being unable to identify the exact source undermines trust in a relationship. Before you know it, intimacy wanes. Communication shuts down. Distance becomes the new norm.

The good news is that there is a solution: *forgiveness*. While anger breeds death in a relationship, forgiveness fosters life. It instills hope and reconciliation. Forgiveness opens the lines of honest communication. Forgiveness allows people to discover new depths of understanding in each other. Forgiveness is the Miracle-Gro for love; when it is added to a relationship, new life and excitement and energy can't help but abound.

Allowing the Light Back In

I have personally experienced the bondage and darkness of unforgiveness and have been set free by practicing forgiveness. Forgiveness comprises three things: (1) *being untied from* the pain of feeling hurt, fearful and frustrated; (2) *pardoning* all the sins acted against us by others; and (3) *treasure hunting* the results of pain experienced over time.

Forgiveness is the antidote to the bondage of destructive anger. In fact, the word "forgiveness" in Greek is actually two words put together: "being released" and "being pardoned." When we release someone from an offense and pardon them, we become freer ourselves.

So how do you foster forgiveness in your marriage? Here are three essential ingredients:

1. Recognize the Sin in Your Own Life

I am 67 years old. That means that I have 67 years in my portfolio of offending people and committing sins. Yet God has faithfully forgiven me for every single one. If God has been so generous with me, how can I not be generous in forgiving others—including my spouse?

Focusing on the sins or faults of others always intensifies anger; but focusing on your own sins or faults diminishes it. In Matthew 18, Jesus tells the story of a guy who owed a big debt—we're talking a boatload of money—and begged for forgiveness. He was released from his debt, but he then forgot the kindness that had been shown to him and placed someone in prison who owed him only a small amount of money. When the guy to whom he owed a lot of money found out about his lack of mercy, he placed the unforgiving man in prison until everything was paid off. God says that's how He looks at our hearts when we are unwilling to forgive others.

No matter how delightful and perfect your relationship with your spouse may be, your marriage will always be a place where God will mature you. There will be times when you are angry with your spouse. The question is, How will you respond? Will you respond with anger or with loving forgiveness? Will you respond by getting mad or by offering the same forgiveness with which you have been forgiven?

2. Pardon the Person Who Has Angered You

Our first 18 months of marriage was complete chaos. The Smalley home was not a peaceful place. The hardest part was that we went through the entire first year thinking that we had to keep tabs on what the other person did wrong. We didn't know about the importance of pardoning each other.

Pardoning someone is not the same as saying that the incident never happened. Pardoning is acknowledging that something *did* happen, but that you are not going to hold the person liable any longer. Pardoning is an act of the will. When you pardon, you fulfill the Lord's prayer to forgive those who trespass against you. Why is this so important? The Bible says that if you don't forgive those who trespass against you, your heavenly Father will not forgive you. In other words, unforgiveness blocks our relationship with God.

Pardoning means erasing the things that you're holding against the other person off of the chalkboard of your heart. You don't have to feel like doing it. You don't have to want to do it. You just do it.

I remember a particularly sticky time in ministry when I was an absolute mess. Nothing was coming together. Relationships were splintering. Unforgiveness ran amuck. In my quiet time, I got down on my knees and began forgiving others and asking God for forgiveness. I spent as much as three hours on my knees, clearing the names and incidents before God, one by one, from the chalkboard of my heart. I forgave the guy who belittled me all the time. I forgave the guy who had cut my salary without saying anything. I forgave the woman who had been so controlling.

During those three hours, I was a basket case before God. I cried. I felt heavy and burdened. I was broken. At the end, I felt only a little better; and it wasn't until weeks later that I felt truly free. That's when I knew that the ropes tying my heart to unforgiveness had completely fallen off.

Pardoning is an act of your will; it's not something you have to feel like doing. This simple prayer can change everything:

Lord, I release this person. I pardon their trespasses, because I'm a trespasser too. I'm a sinner. Thanks for forgiving me; thanks for forgiving them; and thank You, Lord, for giving me the power to forgive this person. Amen.

3. Create a List of Benefits from Your Suffering

Every offense is like a rock hitting you. It hurts. It frustrates. It causes fear. What I now realize is that every offense is also an invitation to grow in God. There are benefits (rewards) within every bad thing that happens to us.We are invited to mature, to blossom in the fruit of the Spirit and become more like Christ.

Here are some of the verses that have meant the most to me:

Hear me, you who know what is right, you people who have my law in your hearts: Do not fear the reproach of men or be terrified by their insults (Isa. 51:7).

Provide for those who grieve in Zion—to bestow on them a crown of beauty instead of ashes, the oil of gladness instead of mourning, and a garment of praise instead of a spirit of despair. They will be called oaks of righteousness, a planting of the LORD for the display of his splendor (Isa. 61:3).

Being confident of this, that he who began a good work in you will carry it on to completion until the day of Christ Jesus (Phil. 1:6).

Be joyful always; pray continually; give thanks in all circumstances, for this is God's will for you in Christ Jesus (1 Thess. 5:16-18).

God turns ashes to beauty, sorrow to gladness. He turns us into oaks of righteousness through our sorrows. I now know that when I am hurt by someone and tempted to take offense, I always have a choice: I can either harbor the hurt or I can forgive.

When we allow anger to remain in our heart, we block one of the most important attitudes that brings the most healing to our bodies and minds: gratefulness. But when we choose forgiveness, we can find the real treasure, the diamond hidden within the offense. Every offense has a jewel inside.

Treasure hunting the bad things that have happened to you and turning those unpleasant experiences into treasures, such as more love and power, in your life is what brings lasting gratefulness.

I (Gary) have come to a place in my own life where I start giving God thanks almost immediately for allowing difficult experiences into my life; because when I do, I instantly receive more of His power, love and other godly qualities through those trials.

Just take a closer look at 2 Corinthians 12:9-10 and Romans 5:3-5. If you memorize these powerful verses and meditate on them day and night until they reach your heart as deep beliefs, you'll be as amazed as I am at how worry and stress fade away and are replaced with a deep sense of gratefulness toward God, and life itself. Even worry has almost disappeared for me through those verses when I add Philippians 4:6-9 to my memory file. There is nothing like being free from anger, worry and fear; and through the heart of gratefulness God is giving me week after week, all three are fading away.

When you begin to look for the benefits or rewards of a trial, you grow into the fullness of love. You become more patient. You become more kind. You become more compassionate, sensitive and aware. You'll see yourself wanting to hug people. You'll cry more easily.

Search the Scriptures for some verses (you can use a Bible concordance for easy access by topic) that remind you of the deeper work God is doing in your life, and memorize and meditate on them.

Maintaining the Light of Forgiveness

Maintaining an open spirit of forgiveness in a marriage takes work every single day. Left unchecked, *Holy Shipwreck!* You are headed for disaster.

On a recent retreat, I (Ted) witnessed one of the greatest icebreakers I had ever encountered at a weekend marriage getaway. Each couple was given two plain T-shirts on Friday night and asked to design shirts that best told the story of their marriage. At first I thought the idea was a bit corny; but on Saturday morning, I laughed and I cried at more than 50 couples sharing the images on their shirts.

I'll never forget how ruthlessly the attendees laughed at Jeff and Sherry. As they stood up, all we could see on their shirts were two feet. No words. No colors, just a plain Sharpie outlining their feet.

Jeff started out. "Hi, we're Jeff and Sherry, and we have been married for 11 years." He spoke with a humble voice and eyebrows raised toward his bride.

"Aaww," the crowd sighed.

"For the past 11 years, we have given each other 30-minute foot rubs every night," he explained.

In disbelief, the crowd started heckling them. I heard guys saying things like, "You've got to be kidding me." "No way!" "Where does he find the time?" "Weird!"

Jeff did not miss a beat during the 60 seconds he was given to explain their shirts. With his chest out, he continued, "That hour every night has fueled our marriage. We know it is the key to a great relationship."

Let me ask you a question: Do you think the key to a great marriage is relaxed feet? Some of you are saying, "Yes!" But seriously, do you think Jeff and Sherry's marriage has been solidified by years of massage therapy?

The answer is no. But I do think that the foot rubs represent something deeper that was happening in Jeff and Sherry's marriage, whether they realized it or not. Though I never had the chance to get the details about where they came up with the idea, foot rubs in a marriage bear a striking resemblance to something Jesus instructed His disciples to do

In John 13, we read about Jesus enjoying His final meal with the disciples. Jesus got up from the table, poured water into a basin and began washing His disciples' feet. When He had finished, He returned to the table.

"Do you understand what I have done for you?" He asked them. "You call me 'Teacher' and 'Lord,' and rightly so, for that is what I am. Now that I, your Lord and Teacher, have washed your feet, you also should wash one another's feet. I have set you an example that you should do as I have done for you. I tell you the truth, no servant is greater than his master, nor is a messenger greater than the one who sent him. Now that you know these things, you will be blessed if you do them" (John 13:12-17).

Though Jeff and Sherry did not use a basin of water, their nightly foot rubs still took on the nature of what Jesus was describing: They were faithfully serving each other. The act of rubbing each other's feet is very personal and intimate. Undoubtedly, if Jeff and Sherry had disagreements or leftover contention from the day, this was their time to sort through it and discuss it in a loving way.

Through the years, we have heard countless stories about how couples have maintained their marriages and an open spirit. For some it was foot rubs; but for others it included the following actions:

1. **Write notes**—We know of one couple who has written a note to each other every day for the past 25 years. Some days they are short and simple; but the continued effort to communicate helps the couple maintain an open posture in their marriage.

2. **Remember your date night, and keep it holy—** Couples who enjoy a regular date night often maintain deeper levels of communication and openness. Date night gives couples time to connect, discuss issues and enjoy each other. Especially if you have children, we cannot encourage you enough to get a sitter, pick a restaurant and make time to talk. Place it on your weekly schedule along with soccer, dance class and swimming lessons. Your relationship will thrive because of it.

3. **Phone home while on the road—**For couples who have to spend time apart because of work and travel, making time to connect—and I mean really connect—while on the road is essential. Amy and I have had to "make up" more on the phone than anywhere else. Leaving home with kids to get ready or dealing with work problems can be quite stressful. Many times the exchange of words can be short, sarcastic or insensitive. A quick phone call two to three minutes from home says "I'm sorry" and keeps accounts short; and times in the evening to talk go a long way toward keeping the connection strong.

4. **Talk pillow talk—**Go to bed early, before exhaustion sets in. Some of the sweetest con-

versations flow right before bed. Warning: Children may result from this one.

5. **Feed the kids early**—For parents with young children, it's important to remember that not every meal needs to be eaten with your kids. While family meals are important, Amy and I have come to the point where we've realized that not every night needs to be family dinner night. Some of our best conversations take place over dinner on nights when we feed the kids their dinner before ours and then send them to the play room. This is a rarity, but it makes for a nice change of pace.

6. **Don't bring everything home**—While this will differ from couple to couple, it's important for those who work outside the home not to bring the stress of their job home. And while it's important to maintain an honest and open relationship with your spouse, communication isn't an excuse for dumping on your partner. Pastor Ted Burden at Woodland Hills Church in Branson is my hero on this one. He shares very little about the behind-the-scenes stuff at church with his wife, Jo. I can't begin to tell you how much peace that creates at home. He is the best at guarding his wife's heart.

Creating a satisfying and fulfilling marriage is a lot like working on a puzzle: You may have all the pieces, but you still have to figure out how they fit together. Forgiveness helps every piece fit together tighter and more smoothly.

A Walk from Darkness into Light

You may be wondering what happened to my (Gary's) friend Larry, whose childhood with an abusive father we touched on earlier in this chapter. Well, Larry and I started working through his issues with his father.

I remember asking him how much of the fault was his father's and how much was his own. Larry admitted that while he was 10 percent in the wrong, his father was clearly 90 percent in the wrong. The numbers weren't really important, but it was important that Larry was willing to take some responsibility.

His father was still alive, so I encouraged him to visit with his dad and make his 10 percent right. Larry flew back to his home in Pennsylvania. He took a walk with his father in a field near their home. Along the way, he put his arm around his dad. (Larry's dad wasn't a particularly touchy person.)

"I did a lot of things wrong when I was in high school and stuff at home, and I'd just like to ask you to forgive me," he said.

Though his father didn't really respond, Larry could feel a transformation in his own heart. He felt lighter and more free than he could ever remember.

A short time later, Larry and I were out shopping together for Christmas presents when we received a call that his mother had died unexpectedly of a heart attack. Larry loved his mother dearly, and he jumped on the first available plane home.

At two in the morning on the eve of the funeral, Larry woke to hear his father crying. He walked into his father's bedroom and knelt down next to him. "I know you're really hurting," Larry said softly.

"I miss your mom so much," his dad said, sobbing. "Larry, do you think you could ever find it in your heart to forgive me for what I did to you and the kids and Mom?"

"I forgive you, Dad."

Shortly after, Larry had the privilege of leading his father to Christ. Over the last 10 years, I have watched Larry and his father hug each other, spend time together and enjoy each other. The relationship has been restored—and it all began with forgiveness.

So here's what we'd like to ask you to do:

1. Can you think of anybody you have offended, and from whom you need to seek forgiveness because you may be contributing to their living in darkness?

2. Can you think of someone you need to go to?

From GarySmalley.com

Q: *I love reading these Q-and-As. Being a newlywed, it is so great to hear the experiences of others. Many of the questions are from individuals with big problems. My issues seem so small in comparison. I'm struggling with the little things, like small frustrations toward my husband. Any advice on getting over my mini-irritations?*

A: Often the very thing that irritates us about others is something we do ourselves or we do that is similar to it. I find it easier to excuse myself than to excuse others. Sure, I have this annoying little habit of biting my nails, but when I'm under a lot of pressure, it calms my nerves. I have a reasonable excuse for doing what I do. But there's no excuse for you smacking your gum. How does that help anything? You should close your mouth while you chew.

Subconsciously, I know my behavior needs correcting, but I don't want to open that can of worms. When my behavior scrapes against yours and causes friction, it's a lot easier to correct your behavior than to change mine.

The problem is often even worse. We easily get bent out of shape over a very minor fault in our mate while harboring and ignoring a major fault in our own life. Jesus noted this tendency when He said:

> Do not judge, or you too will be judged. For in the same way you judge others, you will be judged, and with the measure you use, it will be measured to you.

Why do you look at the speck of sawdust in your brother's eye and pay no attention to the plank in your own eye? How can you say to your brother, "Let me take the speck out of your eye," when all the time there is a plank in your own eye? You hypocrite, first take the plank out of your own eye, and then you will see clearly to remove the speck from your brother's eye (Matt. 7:1-5).

Jesus knows us pretty well, doesn't He? We see a little speck of sawdust or a tiny splinter in our mate's eye and it bugs us no end. We make it our job to get that thing out of there. But all the while, we have this big plank, or maybe even an enormous log, stuck in our own eye, and we don't even notice it.

Allow your frustrations to teach you about yourself. Have as much patience with your husband's irritations as you do with your own.

Answers to the Biggies

I (Gary) have heard stories of a dad forgiving the drunk driver who took his daughter's life. I've visited with a family who forgave the man who murdered their son; and I've sat with the father who molested his own daughter and was forgiven by her later in life. All of these cases go way beyond the marital spat or harsh word spoken. I have wrestled with the "how" behind a man or woman's ability to forgive the "biggies."

In the fall of 2005, my wife, Norma, was the victim of a crime. To make matters worse, I was out of town. She was alone.

It all started when the sound of glass breaking downstairs jolted her awake. Norma jumped out of bed and immediately checked to see if the bedroom door was locked. It was. Soon she heard more noises, first the sound of someone screaming, then moments later something like an eerie chant. She was terrified.

"Please, Lord," she prayed under her breath, "let this be a joke." But it certainly didn't have the feel of a joke. And it wasn't. In the early morning hours, a man had broken into our home. As we discovered later, he had overdosed on methamphetamines and was having a drug-induced psychotic episode. (A year later he was sent to a criminal mental health institute.)

This man had jumped off of his 16-foot balcony and shattered his ankle. He limped across the street, dragging his foot behind him and crashed through our garage window, falling hard on the glass and debris and cutting himself severely. But he felt no pain because of the methamphetamines. Bleeding profusely, he broke through the garage door and entered our home. He was convinced that demons were out to kill him as he careened through our house, knocking over furniture and wrecking our decor. From where Norma hid, the noise sounded deafening. She was sure that he would find her; it was simply a matter of time.

As fear tightened its grip on her, she did the exact thing TV talk show hosts had taught her to do: She ran into the bathroom and locked herself in the toilet area. The intruder would have to break through three heavy doors to get to her. Norma then dialed 911. (I am so thankful we followed through on installing a phone in our bathroom!) Within three minutes, a police officer arrived, but he couldn't enter our home because he wasn't sure how many people were inside. He needed backup. So he waited in our driveway for additional officers to show up.

Meanwhile, Norma endured 20 minutes of the man's screaming, chanting and destroying our stuff—the longest 20 minutes of her life. Several times she heard him screaming so close by that she was terrified he was about to burst through the door of our bedroom. "He's coming in, he's coming in!" she cried to the 911 operator. The operator reassured Norma that the police were ready to burst in if he actually entered the bedroom.

Ultimately, the deranged man barricaded himself against his demons inside the closet of a second-floor bedroom—the room right above Norma. When the police finally apprehended him, they found blood on the door handle of our bedroom. He had ventured all the way to our bedroom door, but for some reason he had stopped. Norma believes to this day that God's angels stood there with their hands outstretched, telling him that he could go no further.

On that October night, Norma's worst fears were realized. But while the events changed my wife and her ability to feel safe alone, she amazed me by how quickly she went into ministry mode. She actually developed a heart of compassion for this man. I can remember her calling Ted to see if the church could help the family. Norma wanted to buy the man's family groceries and wanted someone from the church to deliver them. She asked our pastors to visit him to share the Good News with him, and they did.

Norma has never had the chance to meet this assailant face to face, so the words "I forgive you" have never been spoken. But I don't know if they need to be. Norma's actions and outreach to this man and his family have spoken far more about her spirit of forgiveness than words ever could.

Those 20 minutes forever changed the way I schedule my ministry trips; we even moved out of that home. Norma does not rest as easy at night, but her heart is at rest. She has taken that experience and is using it to start each morning with the praise song that goes, "This is the day that the Lord has made; I will rejoice and be glad in it . . ."

People have a lot of questions when it comes to the issues of conflict, anger and forgiveness. Like Norma, your story is probably personal when it comes to this issue. You may have had something awful happen to you that few others have ever experienced. You may be wondering, *What about in my case?* or *What about in this instance?*

The truth is that no matter how horrific your experiences, if you keep anger in your heart, it will only hold you hostage to the person or event. The only way to be set free is through forgiveness. So no matter what has happened to you, no matter what you've experienced, we urge you to forgive—not so much for them, as for you.

In the upcoming pages, we want to share with you some of the questions we are asked whenever we talk about anger and forgiveness. Our hope and prayer for you is that you will let go of the anger in your life and embrace forgiveness for yourself and those who have done you harm.

Q: *My anger has become a problem. I am explosive at home. My wife says I bring all the frustration from my job home and take it out on the kids and her. I do not want to do this. Can you help me understand anger? Also, what verses can I begin meditating on to help resolve my anger?*

A: Anger is an emotion that is triggered by a number of other feelings. The main three emotions triggered are fear, frustration and hurt feelings. You become angry when you feel rejected, judged, controlled, cheated, misunderstood or like a failure. The trigger for anger is different for each one of us, but keep this in mind: Anger is not sin. It is what you get angry about and what you do with your anger that brings about sin. That is why Scripture says, "In your anger do not sin: Do not let the sun go down while you are still angry" (Eph. 4:26).

There are three approaches you can take when it comes time to deal with anger: You can stuff it, spew it or study it (see chapter 2 for more on this concept). There are plenty of times when we get angry about the right stuff, but we don't handle it in an appropriate way. Ask a trusted friend to help you be accountable regarding your anger issues, and do not give full vent to your anger onto your family. Then you will be well on your way to resolving your anger issue.

Q: *I just finished reading* DNA of Relationships. *When you speak of "walls" being built between people who are in conflict, I thought of many walls between my husband and me. When I tried to share this with him, he said, "Don't believe what people say about walls, because the Bible does not speak of walls between people." My husband said I should not have walls. Is this "wall" concept biblical?*

A: Genesis 3:10 paints a pretty clear picture of a wall: "I was afraid . . . so I hid." Adam and Eve feared the consequences of their actions and in turn tried to put a wall between themselves and God. Do you have emotional distance between you and your husband? Are there any issues that you avoid in your marriage? Do the issues of sex, money or jobs get avoided in your marriage? Do you find yourself avoiding certain subjects for fear of confrontation?

Why do couples get so exhausted in marriage? Because they spend so much energy trying to hide. We put up walls and try to project an image we think our mate wants so that when they look at us, they like what they see. That's a problem, of course, because it's hard for your mate to get close to you if you're standing on the other side of a thick wall or behind a false mask.

The good news is that you can create an open atmosphere that will allow you to be your true self. The apostle Paul put it this way: "We refuse to wear masks and play games. . . . Rather, we keep everything we do and say out in the open, the whole truth on display, so that those who want to can see" (2 Cor. 4:2, *THE MESSAGE*). Paul was not going to allow walls to hinder the gospel. He recognized the potential of walls, and took personal responsibility to remove them.

If you are like me, you long for a marriage in which you feel completely safe, no walls allowed. You want to feel free to open up and reveal who you really are, knowing that your mate will still love, accept and value you no matter what. But too often you and I are hopelessly stuck, afraid to open up with others because we're not quite sure what they will say or do or how they'll use what they learn about us.

Does the Bible speak of walls between people? Absolutely! The biggest "wall" that runs throughout all of Scripture is called *sin*. "The trouble is that your sins have cut you off from God" (Isa. 59:2, *TLB*). "If we say that we never sin, we are only fooling ourselves, and refuse to accept the truth"

(1 John 1:8, *TLB*). Every human on the planet has to deal with this wall called sin. But how? The answer is Christ. "The wages of sin is death, but the gift of God is eternal life through Jesus Christ our Lord" (Rom. 6:23). Jesus Christ said, "I am the way, the Truth, and the Life. No one comes to the Father, except through me" (John 14:6).

Q: *Must I forgive someone who feels they have done nothing wrong?*

A: When it comes to the command to forgive, the Bible is very obvious about what is expected of followers of Jesus Christ:

> Therefore, if you are offering your gift at the altar and there remember that your sister or brother has something against you leave your gift there in front of the altar. First go and be reconciled to your brother, then come and offer your gift (Matt. 5:23-24).

Is anyone excluded from receiving our forgiveness? According to Matthew 5:44-48, even our enemies are worthy of forgiveness:

> But I tell you: Love your enemies and pray for those who persecute you, that you may be sons of your Father in heaven. He causes his sun to rise on the evil and the good, and sends rain on the righteous and the unrighteous. If you love those who love you, what reward will you get? Are not even the tax

collectors doing that? And if you greet only your brothers, what are you doing more than others? Do not even pagans do that? Be perfect (mature), even as your heavenly Father is perfect.

What a verse! What a message! This touches on the very nature of our incredible God who is merciful and gracious to all. Christ was willing to love those who were unlovable. He cared for the prostitutes, thieves and, yes, even tax collectors. Following Christ means that we must learn to forgive those who most offend us. Why our enemies? Because God knows how much unresolved anger kills the spirit within, and He wants us to be free from regret and guilt.

No one is to be excluded from our forgiveness, even the person who is not asking for your forgiveness.

Q: *For whatever reason, I do not like conflict. I never have and I never will. When my husband and I get into an argument, I tend to get overly upset—even if it's just a small issue. How can I control my anger?*

A: First of all, realize that you have the same response as many people. In fact, 80 percent of women do not like to feel disconnected from others. They don't like to feel as though there is a lack of connection between them and their mate; so even a small sense of disconnection can turn a little argument into a huge fight. In my (Ted's) marriage to Amy, I've seen this firsthand. My wife doesn't want to feel disconnected or rejected. Whenever she feels like one of those things is going on, her emotions escalate. Small issues are magnified and exaggerated. Without realizing it, she assigns motives to my actions and words. If I miss taking the garbage out once in a month, for instance, she might say that I never take the garbage out.

My reaction, on the other hand, is that when I feel controlled, I withdraw. I close my heart and remove myself from the situation . . . which makes my wife feel all the more disconnected and rejected. Now I'm pushing her buttons. Before we realize what has happened, it's like we're caught in a rerun of *Everybody Loves Raymond*, where Raymond is tucked up in a corner and Debra is yelling at him. All Debra wants is to connect with Raymond, and all Raymond wants to do is retreat.

If we're not careful, we can escalate out of control with accusatory statements that put both of us on the defense, or worse, the offense. And if left untempered, an escalation results in an explosion of words that we just can't take back.

Both my wife and I know the biblical instruction not to let the sun go down on our wrath. So when an argument starts after the sun has gone down . . . we know we need to fix things, and fast. The good news is that both of us are aware of our own buttons and tendencies for escalation. All it takes to defuse an argument and bring it back down to size—which is usually minute—is an apology for pushing the other person's button. That apology helps us remember that we're on the same team and that we don't want to hurt one another, intentionally or unintentionally.

So to control your anger, you need to understand what your and your spouse's buttons are. Talk about them. Discuss why they're important to you at a time when things are calm. Then look for ways to avoid pushing your spouse's button and acknowledge when yours have been pushed the next time a conflict arises.

Q: *My husband and I were married almost 10 months ago. It's been a bumpy transition learning to live together and do life together. Sometimes when we're having a fight, I don't know what to do, so I call my mom. This makes my husband really upset. Don't I have a right to call my mom whenever I want?*

A: Yes, you do have the right to call your mom whenever you want, but sometimes you need to give up that right to do what's right for your marriage. We all need mentors and people who can speak wisdom into our lives, but when you're in the heat of the moment, that may not be the best time to pick up the phone. Let me ask you this: When you're calling your mom, are you looking for wisdom or are you looking for an ally?

The Bible makes it clear that a man has to leave his father and mother in order to cleave to his wife. Too often when people are in conflict, one or both of the spouses pick up the phone, call a parent and spew everything that happened in the fight. There is no benefit in that for your marriage or your future together. Instead of looking for allies during a heated argument, look at yourself.

Turn your heart toward God and ask Him for His perspective on the matter. You might be surprised at what God reveals to you through prayer. It's easy to think that the goal of marriage is to make you happy; but the real goal of marriage is to make you holy.

Q: *What if after reading this book I still can't forgive my spouse? What if I still hate my spouse?*

A: Every so often, I have couples who come in and actually use the words "I hate you" to one another. They are undoubtedly wrestling with unresolved anger. At those moments, I remind them that even if in the moment they feel hatred, they still need to love each other. It's not an option if you're a Christian.

---

*No matter how annoying, no matter
how hurtful they are, you can
still learn to love through God's
grace and power.*

In the Sermon on the Mount, Jesus instructed, "You have heard that it was said, 'Love your neighbor and hate your enemy.' But I tell you: Love your enemies and pray for those who persecute you, that you may be sons of your Father in heaven. He causes his sun to rise on the evil and the good, and sends rain on the righteous and the unrighteous. If you love those who love you, what reward will you get? Are not even the tax collectors doing that? And if you greet only your brothers, what are you doing more than others? Do not even pagans do that? Be perfect (complete with love), therefore, as your heavenly Father is perfect" (Matt. 5:43-48).

Jesus is saying there's more to life than just coping or just putting up with someone. Loving the unlovable during their most unlovely moments is a mark of maturity in your life. No matter how annoying, no matter how hurtful they are, you can still learn to love through God's grace and power. The other person may not change, but you will be changed forever. You will be set free. You will grow. You will mature. You will be transformed into who and what God desires you to be. And it all begins with loving the other person and releasing him (or her) from what he's done.

This is where the true Christ-follower rises to the surface. He or she is the one who wants to go the extra mile and not just be nice to nice people, but show kindness and love to the most difficult of people.

When couples come in for counseling who hate each other, I ask them: How would you describe your relationship with God? Is it distant? Is it intimate? Do you ignore Him? Is He the center of your life? Do you know Him personally?

Maybe you are consumed with a try-harder religion. You believe that if you work hard, take care of your duties and watch after your family or others, God will look over your whole life and conclude that you are okay. Perhaps you believe that giving up your bad habits will place you in God's good graces.

A relationship with God is not based on what you abstain from doing. It is not about your best efforts. It is about a God who loves you and wants a relationship with you. In fact, the Bible says that He is a God who is passionate about His relationship with you (see Exod. 34:14). Think about that. How many people are passionate about a relationship with you? Well, the God of the universe is. He loves you right where you are. He loves you despite your past. He wants a relationship with you no matter who you are or what you have done.

How can you have a relationship with God? Through His Son, Jesus Christ. As the Bible says, there is only one God and one Mediator who can reconcile God and people. He is the man Christ Jesus (see 1 Tim. 2:5). We have a natural desire to be independent, to be the master of our own life, to live by our own standards. It's the old look-out-for-number-one attitude. The biblical word for that attitude is *sin*. Our sin cuts us off from God. Every single one of us struggles with this problem. All have sinned; all fall short of God's glorious standard (see Rom. 3:23). Therefore, in and of ourselves, we can never measure up.

Yet the story doesn't end there. Jesus Christ, through His death on the cross, has made it possible for you to be in a relationship with God. The first step is to admit that God has not been in first place in your life. Believe that Jesus died to pay for your sin, and ask Him to forgive you. With that admission, you are given this promise: If you confess your sins to Him, He is faithful and just to forgive you and to cleanse you from every wrong (see 1 John 1:9).

You may be asking, *So, what's the catch?* There is no catch! God's forgiveness is free. We don't deserve it, but God wants to give it to us anyway. If there were a way we could earn it, then Christ's death on the cross would be meaningless. His death paved the way for us to give God all of the credit. God saves us by His special favor when we believe. And we can't take credit for it; it is a gift from God. Salvation is not a reward for the good things we have done, so none of us can boast about it (see Eph. 2:8-9).

If you would like to begin a personal relationship with God today, pray something like this simple prayer as an expression of your decision:

Dear Father, thank You for loving me even when I've been unlovable. You have not been first place in my life until today. I submit my life to You. Thank You for sending Your Son, Jesus, to die on that cross. He took care of my sins. Please forgive me. I want to follow You. Make me a new person. I accept Your free gift of salvation. Please empower me to grow now as a follower of Jesus.

MEDITATIONS FOR
FORGIVENESS

Do not gloat when your enemy falls; when he stumbles,
do not let your heart rejoice.

PROVERBS 24:17

Do not say, "I'll do to him as he has done to me;
I'll pay that man back for what he did."

PROVERBS 24:29

If your enemy is hungry, give him food to eat;
if he is thirsty, give him water to drink.

PROVERBS 25:21

In doing this, you will heap burning coals on his head,
and the Lord will reward you.

PROVERBS 25:22

Do not pay attention to every word people say,
or you may hear your servant cursing you.

ECCLESIASTES 7:21

For if you forgive men when they sin against you,
your heavenly Father will also forgive you.
But if you do not forgive men their sins,
your Father will not forgive your sins.

MATTHEW 6:14-15

Blessed are they whose transgressions are forgiven,
whose sins are covered.

ROMANS 4:7

Bear with each other and forgive whatever grievances
you may have against one another.
Forgive as the Lord forgave you.

COLOSSIANS 3:13

Additional Resources for
From Anger to Intimacy

In the *From Anger to Intimacy Study Guide* and *From Anger to Intimacy DVD*, Gary Smalley and Ted Cunningham go beyond the book and take a deeper, biblical look at the topic of anger and forgiveness in the marriage relationship. What does the Bible say about anger? Does Scripture tackle emotions and how to find forgiveness in our marriages? The study guide and companion DVD are fantastic resources for couples to do together, and they are equally useful for individuals, small groups, pastors and leaders.

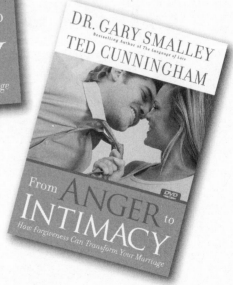

From Anger to Intimacy Study Guide
Gary Smalley and Ted Cunningham
ISBN: 08307.46757
ISBN: 978.08307.46750

From Anger to Intimacy DVD
Gary Smalley and Ted Cunningham
120 minutes
UPC: 607135.015017

The Smalley Relationship Center provides conferences and resources for couples, singles, parents, and churches. The Center captures research, connecting to your practical needs and develops new tools for building relationships.

resources include:

- Over 50 best-selling books on relationships
- Small Group curriculums on marriage & parenting
- Church-wide campaign series with sermon series, daily emails and much more
- Video/DVD series
- Newlywed kit and pre-marital resources

www.garysmalley.com website includes:

- Over 300 articles on practical relationship topics
- Weekly key truths on practical issues
- Daily devotionals
- Conference dates and locations
- Special events
- Weekly newsletter
- Free personality & core fear profiles
- Request a SRC Speaker

To find out more about Gary Smalley's speaking schedule, conferences, and to receive a weekly e-letter with articles and coaching ideas on your relationships, go to www.garysmalley.com or call 1.800.8486329

Attend our live **I Promise Marriage Seminars** taught by

DRS. GARY & GREG
SMALLEY

A six session marriage seminar based on the new
I Promise book and Purpose Driven Curriculum

Free Resources: go to **www.garysmalley.com**

- **Weekly E-letter**

  Receive articles, coaching tips and, inspirational encouragement
  from Gary Smalley which will help you build a more effective and
  stronger marriage.

- **Profiles** ①

  The overall theme of I Promise is security, and you can take a 20 question test on how secure your most important relationship is.

  (Bonus: After you take that profile consider taking our personality
  profile which gives you even more insight into what kind of
  personality styles you andyour spouse fall into.)

Sign up for our FREE

@E-LETTER
WWW.GARYSMALLEY.COM

IN OUR E-LETTER, YOU'LL RECEIVE THE FOLLOWING:

Articles
[Over 300 articles on practical relationship topics]

Key Truths
[Weekly Key Truths on practical issues]

Devos
[Fresh Daily Devotion each day]

Dates & Locations
[Where & when our Seminars are held]

Special Events
[Conferences, Speaking Events, etc.]

Assessments
[Go online to take our free personality and core fear profiles]

Speakers
[Request an SRC Speaker]

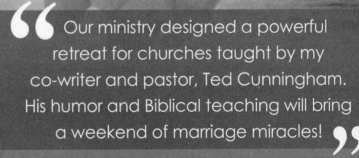

Bring a weekend
of marriage miracles to
YOUR
C H U R C H

"Our ministry designed a powerful retreat for churches taught by my co-writer and pastor, Ted Cunningham. His humor and Biblical teaching will bring a weekend of marriage miracles!"

—Gary Smalley

CONTACT US @
W W W . G A R Y S M A L L E Y . C O M

A Biblical Study of Love, Intimacy, Romance and Sex

There is a secret formula for the best sex of your life, but you won't find the recipe in the pages of a checkout line magazine. Bestselling author Dr. Gary Smalley finally tackles the topic that is on everybody's mind: sex. With his pastor and good friend, Ted Cunningham, Dr. Smalley nudges past our hangups and sacred cows to answer the question, *How can I have the best sex of my life?*

Great sex is made with the same ingredients as a strong and intimate marriage. When we begin with an honest look at the differences between men and women, we can then find ways to bridge the gap and create the honor, intimacy and security that great sex—and a great marriage—need in order to flourish. *The Language of Sex* will give you the secrets to raising the temperature in your relationship outside the bedroom—and in!

The Language of Sex
ISBN 978.08307.45685

The Language of Sex Study Guide
ISBN 978.08307.46101

The Language of Sex DVD
UPC 607135.014775